Behind Closed Doors

A Survivor's Story of the
Boarding School Syndrome

Behind

a survivor's story

Closed

of the boarding

Doors

school syndrome

Mary Fortier

Belleville, Ontario, Canada

Behind Closed Doors
A Survivor's Story of the Boarding School Sydrome
Copyright © 2002, Mary Fortier

ISBN: 1-55306-330-9

All names that are mentioned have been changed to protect the identity of the persons involved. Any similarities are coincidental.

**For more information or
to order additional copies, please contact:**

Mary Fortier
60 Theriault Blvd.
Timmins, ON
(705) 268-9743

Epic Press is an imprint of *Essence Publishing,* a Christian Book Publisher dedicated to furthering the work of Christ through the written word. For more information, contact:
44 Moira Street West, Belleville, Ontario, Canada K8P 1S3.
Phone: 1-800-238-6376. Fax: (613) 962-3055.
E-mail: info@essencegroup.com
Internet: www.essencegroup.com

Printed in Canada
by

To my husband, Terry, who has nourished me with unconditional love and shared his life with me!

To my son, Sean, who has helped me see that even an adult is entitled to tears. Thank you for being my "pride and joy" and giving me time to accept that you're a young man I can be proud of!

Thank you both for the support and strength you gave while I was writing this book!

Table of Contents

$\mathcal{A}$cknowledgements

There are so many special people to thank for the support I received while writing *Behind Closed Doors*.

"Thank you" to my mother, Alexandria, who has healed with me and who, despite many sorrowful trials, is still achieving a positive outcome. Thank you for helping me understand the history of our family.

To my sisters: Vivian, for allowing me to share our memories and include our photos; Theresa, who I think of so often; my late sister, Margaret, who did not see the fulfillment of my promise to publish this manuscript.

To my brothers: George, who has always encouraged and believed in me and my talents; Fred, Edmond, Peter, Johnny, and Michael—thank you for allowing me to draw on our childhood memories!

To my sister-in-law, Linda Sackaney-Chum, for always being so compassionate and understanding.

To my nephew, David John-George, who was always available when I needed help with errands and tasks.

To my mentors: Rachelle Piche, Collet St. Denis, Lynn Ellerton, who all took part as positive role models and helped me see that my qualifications were genuine.

A special thank you to my best friends: Connie McKay, Pat and Larry Lefevre, for their support and prayers, Joan and Bill Hollingshead, for granting me my cyber moccasins.

A special thank you to my sponsors, the Timmins Native Friendship Centre, for accepting responsibility for this project: David Faries, President; David Thomas, Vice-President; Hannah Sutherland, Treasurer; Linda Bates, Secretary; David Wheesk, Director; Conrad Iahtail, Director; Marilyn Sutherland, who provided so much support at the outset of this project.

Thank you to those who sent support letters: Diane Riopel and Hannah Sutherland of the Ojibway and Cree Cultural Centre; Larry Martichenko of Professional Counselling Services; Angie Lafontaine of Misiway Milopemahtesewin Community Health Centre; Bill Gillespie of Kunuwanimano Child and Family Services; Angela Sheeshish and Peter Sackaney, who are also survivors.

Thank you to Gary Farmer, who published and promoted my article in the *Aboriginal Voices: North American Native Magazine*, to Paul Seesequasis of the Ontario Arts Council, for the grant provided as I started writing *Behind Closed Doors*, and to the Aboriginal Healing Foundation, for approving the grant to publish.

Preface

Throughout history and in every generation, Canadian Native people have encountered the dominance of other religious and/or governmental groups. In more recent times, representatives from these groups shared a common vision to destroy Native culture by assimilating it into Euro-Canadian society. Native people were still able to maintain aspects their lifestyle until the federal government of Canada enforced and enacted their paternalistic views in Native education.

In 1870, the federal government realized that day schools on reserves were not as efficient as they had anticipated, because the majority of Natives continued to depend on the seasons to hunt, fish, and trap. Their livelihood required relocating their families for long periods of time which naturally resulted in poor school attendance among Native children. As a result, the federal government began to revamp the education offered to Native children in Canada by showing interest in an industrial school that had served Native children in the United States. In 1879, the government exercised their intentions by assigning Nicholas Flood Davin to inquire after the school and determine if it would be practical for application among Canada's Native children. Upon completion of his inquiry, Davin recommended that the government establish an industrial school similar to the US model, strongly suggesting it be funded by the federal government and supervised by religious orders to ensure directives were enforced and regulated. Unfortunately, Davin chose to conceal that this type of "affiliation" was unsuccessful and aborted by the United States' government.

Evidently, Davin's' report was approved because the industrial school provided an opportunity to assimilate Native children into mainstream society by training them to abandon their culture. It enhanced the vision shared by the federal government and religious orders of the day before Davin's report was submitted. The latter part of Davin's report identified the group to be subjugated by the implementation of the industrial school: "If anything is to be done with the Indian, we must catch him very young" (Agnes Grant, *No End of Grief* p. 64).

The federal government responded by establishing and formalizing two types of schools. The first was a boarding school that served Native boys and girls at elementary levels. The second was a privatized industrial school for Native boys of fourteen to eighteen years, which permitted occasional exceptions to enroll younger boys. Later, the criteria changed to include Native girls. The curriculum provided for both institutions included rudimentary English and French and practical training in agriculture and domestic skills. In addition, these schools were to be operated by collaborating tendering contracts to various religious orders that were permitted to intensify religious training. Subsequently, specific requirements were essential to concoct the operational procedure of these schools. Native children were to be separated from their parents and removed from their natural surroundings. The educational process was subdued to ensure Native children did not advance academically. This procedure continued into graduation to ensure Native students remained in the lower classes of dominant society. The mandate of the schools was outlined in three main objectives: to "convert," "civilize," and "educate" Native children by creating and finalizing a plan to mass-produce students who would adapt to and adopt the lifestyle of Euro-Canadians.

Indian industrial schools, boarding schools, and residential schools were built throughout Canada. This included St. Patrick's (later renamed St. Ann's), located along the coast of James Bay in the remote community of Fort Albany, Ontario, which was occupied by the Cree tribe. The school was owned by the Roman Catholic Church, operated by religious orders of priests, brothers ordained as Oblates of Mary Immaculate, and nuns ordained as Grey Nuns of the Cross, and funded by the federal government. Its doors were opened in 1903 and closed in 1973.

St. Ann's Residential School served Indian boys and girls ranging in age from four to sixteen years. Indian children were forced to leave their homes in Fort Severn, Attawapiskat, Peawanuck (Winisk), Ogoki, Moosonee, Moose Factory, Smooth Rock Falls, Armstrong, Calstock, etc. Some local Indian students from Fort Albany and

Kashewan stayed in the residence on weekdays and were allowed to go home for weekends. Other students attended school during the day and could go home at the end of the day. However, these students were housed during the spring flood. Most of the students from other communities remained on the premises for ten months and returned home for two months of summer vacation. While at school, these children were under the supervision of priests, brothers, nuns, and lay people who completely abrogated parental responsibilities. A majority of the Native children spoke Cree, Oji-Cree, and Ojibway. Many of the non-Native staff learned to speak the Cree language to use it to their advantage.

Some students came from different circumstances. For example, some became orphaned while at school while others were abandoned and forced to stay at the school until adulthood. Some graduates returned home only to find that their newly acquired skills were valueless in their community or that their limited academic achievement was useless in competing for meaningful employment in mainstream society.

Unfortunately, because of the bleak futures they faced, the negative repercussions of this educational experience on Native young people often affected three or four future generations. Some Natives made it to their teens while others died prematurely from suicide or the insidious effects of alcohol and/or drug abuse. In the early 1940s, three Native boys escaped St. Patrick's and chose to die rather than return to the school. Some children survived the system only to suffer the consequences of physical, mental, emotional, sexual, verbal, and spiritual abuses. Many former students spoke of the ordeals but were not heard; some were intimidated into silence and some chose to remain silent. Many, like me, are now disclosing the past love/hate relationships between students and religious orders that have been a part of our history.

This book is not intended to insult or criticize any religion or government that may parallel groups mentioned herein. Rather, it is to promote awareness and educate Canadians as to the difficulties many Native children have suffered in the residential school system. It is meant to encourage Native people who have endured such experiences to grieve and heal in all areas—mental, physical, emotional, and spiritual. It seeks to encourage future generations to inherit our strength by reflecting on the past and admiring the many positive role models who emerged from these struggles.

All scenarios, experiences, and/or solutions are not exhaustive; therefore, one can honestly decide whether residential school syndrome is associated with many societal problems that continue to exist and affect the lives of Natives in a negative way. Chrisjohn states:

> Residential Schools were created out of the largess of federal government and the missionary imperatives of the major churches as a means of Christian civilisation to Aboriginal populations. With the benefit of late - 20th century hindsight, some of the means with which this task was undertaken with the best humanitarian intentions. Now in ant large organisation, isolated incidents of abuse may occur, and in such some Residential Schools now appear to be suffer in low self-esteem, alcoholism, somatic disorders, violent ten-

dencies, and other symptoms of psychological distress (called Residential School). While these symptoms seem endemic to Aboriginal Peoples in general (and not limited to those who attended Residential School), this is likely to have come because successive generations of attendees passed along, as it were, their personal psychological problems to their homes and communities and through factors such as inadequacy of parenting skills, perpetrated the symptomology, if not the syndrome. In order to heal those individuals who still suffer the consequences of their school experiences, if it is necessary and appropriate to establish formally the nature of Residential School Syndrome and causally link the condition to the Residential School abuses (physical, sexual or emotional) determine the extent of its influence in Aboriginal populations and suggest appropriate and community interventions that will bring about psychological and social health.[1]

Although the authors outline the overall picture and there is truth and merit to what they say, their solutions, like mine, are not exhaustive and will not fit everyone. What has worked for me is my Christian faith regarding the differences between spirituality and religion. Spirituality is based on supernatural laws and can exist without religion, whereas religion cannot exist without spirituality and is mainly based on man-made laws.

As a Native person, I have a good understanding of ancient traditions, and if Native traditionalism and Christian spiritualism are practiced with sincerity in their purest forms, they have many parallels.

The benefits I hope people will receive by reading about my experiences are that there is life after residential school, and the key is not to blame others and focus on similarities rather than differences. Whatever one chooses to believe, he or she must practice it in its purest form.

[1] *The Circle Game: Shadows and Substance in the Indian Residential School Experience in Canada.* Roland Chrisjohn and Sherri Young with Michael Maraun. (Quoted as written, spelling errors are original.)

Family History

My ancestors originated in Fort Albany, Ontario, during an era when missionaries came to share their faith. My great-grandmother, Jane, became a converted Roman Catholic. Naturally, her children were baptized in the same religion.

My grandmother, Anna, was born in 1905. In 1910, she became the first family member admitted into St. Patrick's (later renamed St. Ann's Boarding School). She remained there for eight years. Later, she met my grandfather, Albert, who was born in 1898. His parents had maintained their traditions and avoided getting involved with conversion and education. On July 17, 1917, at the age of twenty, he joined the Canadian Expeditionary Forces and served in London, England until his discharge on April 12, 1919. Service records show he was illiterate! Upon his return, he married Anna. They had four children and only one survived—my mother, who was born in 1923. Her name, "Key Shay Peesim," meaning "the

Great Sun," was given in a Cree ceremony. My great-grandmother disapproved of her traditional upbringing.

In 1927, at the age of four, she was admitted into St. Patrick's Boarding School. Mother recalls a priest telling her she had to change her name because it was "demonic." Shortly after, she was baptized and named "Alexandria." Unfortunately, she had to learn to accept more changes than just her name. In 1930, her father died. Two years later, her widowed mother married a man named Peter, of whom her grandmother disapproved because of his reputation as a womanizer. She wanted someone responsible to raise Alexandria.

The new couple had plans that did not include a child. Anna told her daughter she was going down the river to set up a fishing net. She did not return. A couple days later, a priest informed Alexandria he met Anna and Peter paddling down the river. They stopped to talk with him and told him they were on their way to Pagawa, Ontario. Consequently, Alexandria remained at St. Patrick's school for twelve years, because she had been abandoned.

In August 1939, the school burned down. She had just turned sixteen and was homeless. Her grandmother refused to take responsibility for a grown teenager. As with other homeless girls, the priest and nuns arranged a marriage for her. The girls were lined up before the bachelors from the school and village to be selected as wives. My mother was chosen by a man who worked on the ships that transported cargo into other remote communities. After marriage, she took a job at the mission hospital. In 1940, the first of their eleven children was born.

My father's past was mysterious. My paternal grandparents, Sophie and John, came from Attawapiskat,

Ontario. They had ten children. My father, Joseph, born in 1914, remembered traveling with his parents by canoe to Fort Albany. He was placed with his grandparents who were instructed to register him at St. Patrick's Boarding school. He remembered standing along the shore, crying and screaming as he watched his parents paddle down the river, headed back home without him. They ignored his pleas and disappeared over the open water. He entered the school at five and remained there for eighteen years.

Although he had a good relationship with his grandparents, with whom he stayed during summer holidays, he did not have any contact with his immediate family over the years. One day, while I was playing on the floor, I overheard my father talking to my mother. He began to cry when he expressed the pain of being rejected by his family, an event he attributed to a rumour involving his mother. He suspected she had committed adultery and he was the result, which was why his father and siblings constantly mistreated him. In 1929, shortly after the man whom he considered to be his father died, his mother relocated to Fort Albany. By this time, some of his siblings had been placed at St. Patrick's school. My father remained in the boarding school while helping his mother raise five of his siblings. It gave him the opportunity to rebuild his relationship with her, but his siblings did not put much effort into it. When he married Alexandria on December 1, 1939, he instructed his brothers to help their mother raise the remaining four siblings.

Years later, on Halloween night, 1962, my father was killed by a drunk driver. His death was ruled "accidental" and the impaired non-Native driver was released.

My mother requested reasonable financial support for her ten fatherless children as well as the one she was expecting. The Chief and Council did not approve of the idea and never bothered to mention her claim in court. Justice was never satisfied on the behalf of an innocent Native man killed on crown land or his widow and orphaned children.

When my grandmother, Sophie, came to my father's funeral, she cried at the sight of my brother, Johnny, who had a light complexion and a tint of red in his brown hair. She told my mother he was an exact replica of my father as an infant and confessed her relationship with a man employed at the ships of the North Western Company. In this relationship, my father was conceived. My grandfather found out about it and retaliated by openly addressing my father as "bastard" and encouraging his children to mistreat him. Grandma admitted that her son had suffered the consequences of her deceit and betrayal. Unfortunately, the secret my father had questioned most of his life was never revealed before his death.

Like that of many other Natives, my family background unfolded during the era of the government's education-system revamp. Native children were intended to abandon their culture. They were removed from their homes and communities, relocated to boarding schools, placed under the guardianship of incompetent caregivers who were allowed to intensify religion training. Religious text used in small print proudly identifies the ethnic group pinpointed: "A L'Usage Des Sauvages." [1]

Native children learned quickly that rules and regulations were to be upheld. This included moral aspects of the Roman Catholic religion. Failure to comply resulted in harsh punishment. My grandmother informed me that, during her school days, the staff enforced strict rules. One evening, her friends, both male and female, got together to play hide-and-seek. A priest came along and expressed his disapproval of the game by grabbing my grandmother and striking her on the neck with a karate chop. The force knocked her out. Later, the priest confronted her and insinuated they were playing something lustful. My grandmother was never the same after the incident. She became easily intimidated, paranoid, nervous, and fearful.

My grandfather, Peter, described one of his ordeals. One day he was hungry, so he helped himself to an apple. The same priest caught him and instructed my grandfather to follow him to the basement. Once they got there, the priest took rope and tied his wrists. Next, he hooked his tied hands onto a nail that was hammered in beam above so that his arms extended upward. The priest took a whip and flogged his back until he messed his pants. After the punishment, the priest justified his method by saying he was teaching the boy not to steal so he wouldn't go to hell. My grandfather became obsessed with the fear of going to hell.

When my grandmother, Anna, and her peers entered the system, they became known as "products" created by the federal government and the Roman Catholic Church. These institutions soon realized the generation was not prepared for assimilation because they were under-educated and over-converted. My parents' generation became the "descendants." Basic labour and practical skills were offered to the students according to gender. But once again, the federal government and the Roman Catholic Church created a generation of Indians who had an education that was useless in their communities and valueless outside their communities.

Years later, five of my siblings and I entered St. Ann's Residential School. We were baptized in the Roman Catholic religion and given Christian names. We were all English-speaking, illiterate in our Native tongue as reading or writing in Cree syllabic no longer existed. The academic level of the school had improved some. Religious instruction was continued and modernized by way of an animated role model named Bambo, a coloured boy converted to Catholicism. He was used to spy on non-converts, coloured people portrayed as Natives dancing around a campfire. Through several scenes, Bambo kneels in the church, and the priest reads out his small-print prayers addressed to those "heathens," "pagans," "savages," and "devil worshippers." Thus, we became the final generation, the "survivors" of Residential School Syndrome.

---

1 L.J.C.M.I. Recuiel Du Prieres Catechisme et Cantiques: Evangelizare Pauperibus, (possibly) Pauperes Evangelizantur. Montreal Libraire Beauchemin, Limitee. 256 Saint Paul, 1907.

Memories

In 1961, my family moved to Constance Lake, a Cree reserve in Calstock, Ontario. It is located thirty kilometers west of Hearst, along the Highway 11 corridor. Fortunately, we were one tribe that had access to a non-Native town and had some experience in integrating with white people. Before entering the reserve, there was, and still is, a little French settlement passing the railway crossing. On the right side stood a Canadian Railway Station; to the left was a general store. At the opposite side was the main hall that was used as a church, dance and movie hall, and a couple of houses stood nearby. On the main road, going to the left, were Lecour's Lumber and a few houses. Then there was a wooden culvert and, around the bend, Gosselin's Lumber. About a kilometer down the road, it branched out into two directions; right lead to the reserve. Before entering, three houses came into view. My family lived in the third house. Continuing down the road around the corner, was the main center of the reserve:

houses, a Pentecostal Church, an Anglican Church, and, in between, the natural scenery of Constance Lake as well as the community hall and day school.

My fondest memory is of my parents' house, which they shared with ten of their children (six boys—George, James, Fred, Edmond, Peter, and Johnny, and four girls—Margaret, Theresa, Vivian, and me). It was normal to come from a large family and not unusual to live in one small house. Even though our home was not elaborate, my parents were experienced in arranging the accommodations to make it bearable for all of us. There was no electricity or indoor plumbing which was common for homesteads on the reserve. It was the home my father provided for us, a home my siblings and I shared and valued for a short time.

Unexpectedly, our life changed and the change affected us all differently. I can remember my parents and older siblings preparing to get ready for the Halloween party at the community hall. I approached my father as he was helping James get ready for the best-dressed contest. I looked up at him, smiling, and asked, "Daddy, can I come too?"

He returned a loving smile and replied, "When you get a little older." Feeling disappointed, I went to my bed and listened to everyone talking and laughing as they left the house. I was restless and extra sensitive to sounds when my parents were not home. Perhaps it was because I always felt secure in their presence. Within a few hours, I awoke to the voice of my father speaking to my mother about getting some money from his friend. I got excited and ran to him as soon as he opened the door. He scooped me in his arms, embraced me, and said, "Hey! What are you doing up? You're supposed to be sleeping."

I ignored what he said and asked, "Daddy, can I go with you?"

"No, little girls can't go out late at night.Come on, I'll put you back to bed." He put me down to tuck me in. I pushed the blankets away and sat up. He sat on the side of my bed and faced me. "Daddy, can I please go with you?" I asked again.

Suddenly, he looked at me very seriously and took me in his arms. "*Danis* (which means 'daughter'), always remember Daddy loves you very much. But I have to go right now and you can't come with me." He gave me another hug and repeated, "*Danis*, always remember, Daddy will always love you." He stood up, laid me down and tucked me in. He gave me a kiss me on the cheek and said softly, "Go to sleep." As he walked away, he stopped, looked at me and gave me a smile. I became more relaxed and drifted to sleep with my father's voice echoing in my head: "*Danis*, always remember Daddy loves you...."

About an hour later, I awoke to people crying. I got up and saw my older siblings, relatives, and friends scattered in the living room and kitchen. My brother, George, was talking to our cousin, Joe. His facial expression revealed disbelief and horror. In shock, he jumped backward and broke the window, falling out. I noticed my mother sitting alone and my father was nowhere to be seen. I walked towards her and asked, "Mommy, where's Daddy?" She just sat staring at the floor, so I concentrated on finding him.

I proceeded to my parents' bedroom, only to find my sister, Margaret, crying. She extended her arms and I went to her. She was crying and saying, "Mary, Daddy died and he's never coming home!" I pulled away from her, thinking, *"What does 'died' mean? Daddy wouldn't do that."*

The next morning, I woke up to find more people crying and sobbing uncontrollably. I wanted them to stop. Their cries were of such despair it made my heart ache. I got up and continued to look for my father and decided to wait for him. My thoughts were interrupted by a conversation my relatives were having. One said that my parents had been walking about five minutes from our home when an impaired driver lost control of his car and struck my father. I sensed there was something seriously wrong but I could not comprehend what death meant.

The next two days were hectic. I remember watching people crying or walking around in shock, and wondering what was wrong with them. Everyone was dressed in black and preparing to go to church in Hearst. The next thing I recall was standing at the entrance of the church. The bishop caught my attention when I overheard him say, "We can't bring him into the church because he died drunk." I wondered whom he was talking about. I noticed my father's friend looking disgusted and responding through clenched teeth, "He was my best friend. His wife and children are entitled to see him have a decent burial and Mass in church! We're bringing him in whether you like it or not!" It appeared as though the bishop gave in to avoid a scene. I wondered why my father's friend was so upset and angry.

I watched as people entered the church. One of my aunts took me by my hand and led me to a pew. As I sat down, the choir began to sing a heart-wrenching song and the crying started again. I was beginning to feel frustrated because I could not understand why everyone was so upset. My aunt whispered in my ear, "Your Daddy's here." I looked and saw a casket roll slowly by and thought, "*Why is he in there? Daddy! Daddy, wake up!*"

When the service was over, we left the church and proceeded to the cemetery. On our arrival, a strong gust of cold wind brought me back to reality. I watched the pallbearers carry the casket and place it near the hole on the ground. I was stunned when they lowered it into the cold wet hole and watched in horror as someone grabbed a shovel of mud and threw it onto the casket. Others followed with handfuls of mud. Knowing my father was in the casket, I wanted to jump down and protect him, but someone from the crowd took me by the hand and led me away. I kept walking with my head turned to the hole in the ground, inwardly screaming, "*Daddy! Daddy! Wake up! Why do you want to stay in there? You're strong; push it open!*" For the first time, a surge of pain touched my heart. I wanted to cry, scream, and run. Instead, I went numb.

When we got home, everyone was quiet and lost in thought. Once in awhile, someone would break down and cry. Even though the house was packed, it felt empty without the presence of my father. It finally dawned on me that he would not be coming home, even though I didn't understand why. I began to feel alienated and lifeless and remember thinking, "*How can I go on without seeing him?*" As young as I was, memories of him flashed before me. No doubt he had his faults, but I chose to keep the positive memories in my mind and spirit. Like any other child, my father had been my hero and he contributed much to my life.

Teaching through Examples

I was born in 1956, a middle child with six older siblings and five younger. My parents did not have any favorites among us. However, I developed a very strong bond with my father perhaps because he delivered me in our home in Long Lac, Ontario. He was the type of father who looked after his family and would go wherever the jobs were, even if it meant relocating us. Our needs were his primary concern and he knew how to distribute his time among us. He always worked hard and did his best.

My father impressed me in many ways. He was a compassionate person who expressed genuine kindness to those less fortunate. Because he was a skilled hunter, he would sometimes be hired as a guide. If the hunt was a success, he would often refuse to accept money and charge only bullets for his next hunt or a piece of meat for his family. He became well known with seasonal hunters from down south or the United States. They paid him for his services and he usually took their money because he knew they could afford it.

My father believed in cultivating the spiritual lives of his children. He had dreams for us and tightly controlled our home to make sure we were well-mannered and would become respectable young men and women.

As a little girl, I remember being my father's shadow. I watched while he was busy doing chores and loved the quiet we shared as I nestled beside him with my head on his shoulder while he read the Bible. He always tried to blend his beliefs with his actions, and I can recall many scenes in which his character shone through.

Several such scenes took place during hunting season. Whenever my father got a moose, he would prepare the meat, cut it into chunks, and give it away to needy friends and families. Everyone was delighted. On one occasion, I watched him place the moose bones neatly on a log rack which he had built between two trees. "Daddy," I asked, "why are you putting the bones up there?"

He looked over at me and smiled, "To show respect to the Great Spirit, so next time I go hunting he will provide me with another moose so I can feed my family and share it with my friends." As young as I was, that response took root in my spirit.

My father was the type of person who believed in encouraging others to help themselves. In another scene, I was sitting nearby, watching him split wood. A man came by and asked my father for a meal. My father looked at him and said, "Tell you what. Go see my wife in the house. She has something cooked up. Eat and come help me chop this wood." The man agreed. When he had finished eating, he returned to help my father. He looked my way and said, "That's a cute little girl you have there."

My father responded, "Thank you. She has a way of attracting a person's eye. I think it's her dark complexion and big brown eyes. She's my tar baby!" They looked at each other and started laughing.

A little later, I saw a big mountain of freshly chopped wood. My father's face shone with delight, pleased that a major chore was completed. The man thanked my him for the meal and walked away. My father said, "Not so fast!" and reached into his pocket and handed the man $25. "It's not much, but it should help you for awhile."

The man looked surprised. "I wasn't expecting anything, but this is plenty!" He shook my father's hand. I remember standing beside my father and discerning he had done something good. I raised my arms for him to pick me up. As he held me, he said, "*Danis*, when you grow up, always feed someone who is hungry, and whenever you can afford to pay someone for work, give your best!" We stood and watched the man waving at us as he walked away.

My father never expressed his feelings, except when his children got hurt. Then he could not hide the pain he felt, especially when he couldn't do anything about it. In one scene, my brother, Edmond, my cousin, Don, and I were playing with an axe. Don ordered me to put my doll Gumbi on a chopping stump so he could decapitate it. I reluctantly agreed but warned him that I would put my hand on it to save it. He refused to take my threat seriously. I watched as he swung the axe in the air. I noticed it coming down. Thinking I was performing a heroic act, I quickly placed my hand over it. The next thing I knew, my fingers were dangling and blood was gushing out! In horror, I screamed and froze on the spot. My parents were watching in shock. Suddenly, my father came racing towards me, cursing in Cree all the way. He scooped me up and carried me into the house. My mother grabbed anything in view to wrap my hand. No matter what she did, my blood kept seeping through the material. Through the whole ordeal, an argument erupted. I remember my mother screaming at my father, "I'm taking her to the doctor. She will grow up and get married one day, and she will need her hand." In the meantime, I clung tightly to my father, crying and screaming with my face snuggled between his neck and shoulder. He said he was going to get the taxi to drive us to the doctor's place, but I refused to let go of him. My mother had to literally pry me away. Then I clung tightly to her and would not let go. My mother instructed my brother, George, to hold me. He too had to pry me away. When I got ahold of him, I hung on, still crying and screaming. By this time, George was emotional; he kept repeating through a quavering voice, "It's okay! My girl, it's okay." My father came rushing in but I could not let go of George. He had to yank me away.

When we arrived at Dr. Mackey's office, he took one look at my hand and doubted he would be able to stitch the fingers back properly. He spoke with my parents and informed them of what he suspected would happen: my fingers could be amputated, two of my fingers could become maimed, or my whole hand could become permanently maimed. The atmosphere was somber. My father stood by me as I lay screaming and crying on the examination table. He kept consoling and coaching me not to move as the doctor proceeded to stitch my hand. For the first time, I noticed tears forming in my father's eyes; they gave me the impression he felt helpless. When the doctor was done, he instructed my parents to take me to Thunder Bay.

I drifted in and out of consciousness on the train. Once I was admitted to the hospital, I underwent intensive reconstructive surgery on my hand. My parents were disappointed to hear that it would be permanently scarred but grateful it would not be maimed. When I returned home, everyone encouraged me to exercise my hand. They made sure the dressing was cleaned and changed daily. After a couple of weeks, it was completely restored! Even the scars eventually healed.

For the longest time, I suffered extreme fear whenever I saw the axe. My father never forced me to get over it but was patient and understanding. One day, while he and I were outside, he went into the wood shed. I was afraid to follow as I knew the axe was stored there. However, I wanted to be with him so much, I reluctantly entered the shed. He started explaining very gently how valuable the axe was as a tool. He put it down and came towards me. He took me by the hand and led me to the axe. As he was talking, he put my hand on the handle of the axe. When he noticed he had made progress, he took me in his arms and hugged and kissed me. At end the lesson, he joked, "It's not used for chopping little girl's fingers!"

Like any other parent, my father cared enough to apply discipline when necessary. I remember once when he was upset with me for misbehaving. For my punishment, he ordered me to sit at the table and not move until he said so. I took him seriously and did not dare disobey. Eventually, everyone was in bed. I remained on the chair, listening to the snoring. I was beginning to feel tired, so I folded my arms, leaned on the surface of the table and rested my head. Finally, my father got up in the dark to put wood into the stove. I startled him when I asked, "Daddy, can I go to bed now?"

He looked surprised and started laughing. "*Danis*," he said, "I forgot all about your punishment." He felt so bad, he carried me into his bed. I remember my parents giggling as I drifted into sleep.

I also my father's sense of humour at good timing. In one particular scene, it was Peter's birthday. Father got all his children to sing "Happy Birthday" repeatedly as he paraded Peter back and forth. When I got bored, I asked if I could go and play outside. I recall taking my stuffed cloth doll, which had a pointy head and a plastic face, outside with me. I sat her on a chair and turned away. Suddenly, a black crow swooped down, scooped up my doll, and flew away. I started crying and my parents and siblings came running to check on me. All I was able to do was point at the crow flying away with my doll. Everyone could not help but laugh. My father picked me up to console me. He said, "It's okay! I'll buy you another one." I felt sad for my doll yet it looked so comical seeing her dangle from the crow's beak. I cried and laughed at the same time. Suddenly, my father pointed and said, "Your doll is going to heaven!" We all started laughing.

Family events were precious to my father. He would spend time with his older children by taking them to a movie or, in the winter, slide with them. Other times, outings included all family members. One such occasion was Treaty Day, celebrated on July first. At our last outing together as a family, my parents took us to the fair for children's activities. I can still remember admiring and smiling at my father for riding with my brother, Johnny, on a merry-go-round. When the events of the day were over, they would have one of the older siblings care for us and take an evening out with other couples. On these outings, I could never comprehend why my parents returned smelling awful, looking dizzy, and singing Christmas carols in the summer!

My father also took his responsibility for the family seriously. He always got job, even if he had relocate us. At one of these times, he sheltered us in a tent until there was a vacancy for a house. When we finally got one, my mother was so excited she decided to move in while Father was at work. My brothers, Fred and James, were her main helpers. She had warned the boys to watch out for the freight trains that went by periodically. My brothers proceeded to move the boxes containing clothes. They became over-confident and decided to take a box across the tracks. In the middle of the track, they heard the train whistle blow and panicked and dropped the box. I remember a loud pop and the sight of clothes flying everywhere. The funniest part was seeing my father's brand new long johns fly upward and land sprawling across the engineer's window. We laughed uproariously. When my mother and her helpers regained their composure, she instructed us not to say anything about it. My father noticed we were grinning more then usual when he got home. But when winter rolled around, we had to tell him why his long johns went mysteriously missing!

My father was supportive of my mother when it came to the children. If she was busy, he did his best to assist her. I remember feeling insecure on my first day of school. The day school was about fifteen minutes from our home.

As we walked hand in hand, I looked up at my father and asked, "Daddy, why do I have to go to school?"

He answered, "*Danis*, school is going to be a major part of your life. You have to go. It's part of growing up."

"Daddy, I'm scared. I want to stay home with you and Mommy."

"Don't be scared," he said. "There will be other little boys and girls there. You're going to make friends and you will get used to it." He stopped and picked me up. "There are two things I expect of my children. They will either be educated or become working-class people. You, my girl, will make something of yourself."

I hugged him and said, "Okay, Daddy, but will you stay with me there?"

He laughed. "I can't, but the morning will go by so fast, you won't even notice it. I promise I'll come for you as soon as school is over." Before we arrived at the school, he put me down and said, "Walk like a big girl now." I wanted him to be proud of me so I obeyed. Deep down, I wanted to cry and remember thinking, "I don't want to grow up. It's nicer being with Daddy." He escorted me to the door where we were greeted by a teacher. My father said, "I'll come back later." He nudged my shoulder into the classroom. The teacher gave me a desk by one of the windows and I saw him walk away.

The Grieving Child

When my father died, I entered the grieving process without knowing it. I locked the memories in my mind and engraved the loss on my heart. At the time, I did not understand what I was experiencing. All I knew was that the hurt and pain I felt were genuine. My mother noticed I would withdraw at times and become despondent. Talking and laughing, actions that had come easily to me, became less frequent and more difficult. I changed from a very extroverted girl to a very introverted one. I could not comprehend the reality of my father's death, nor did I possess ability to accept something I could not understand. I figured his absence would be temporary.

With a house full of children, my mother sensed I was slipping away. She became more concerned when my nose would bleed for no apparent reason. She would get my brother to hold me in his arms and tilt my head back. George would gentle assure me, saying, "It's okay, my girl, things are going to get better." I would lie still and wait for the bleeding to stop. Deep inside, I was crying, *"I want Daddy to come home because I miss him."* George always managed to comfort me.

At other times, I became violently ill for no reason. A fever would rise, and I would be weak and dizzy. It happened so many times, my mother sat by looking helpless. I used to feel bad because I could not explain the feelings of isolation and desertion that resulted from my father's death.

I believe my mother knew I was grieving, because she was really supportive. She got my older siblings to spend time with me. One day, I heard her express concern to my oldest sister, Margaret. She said, "There's something wrong with Mary. She hasn't been the same since...."

Margaret interrupted her. "I know. Since Dad died."

"I need to spend more time with her alone," Mother answered. This she managed to do without neglecting her other children. She would take me on walks, visits to her friends, and sometimes to the store for a pop or ice cream.

One day, my mother said, "I have a surprise for you! Margaret is going to babysit while we go to a movie!" I was delighted and honoured to be going out with my mother. Father's words came back to me: "When you get a little older, you will be able to go out at night." Mother and I walked hand in hand down the road that I had walked so many times with my father. For the first time in months, I felt secure.

The movie was *Kissing Cousins*, starring Elvis Presley. I sat quietly during the whole thing. In one scene, an old lady started singing and crying because she thought her husband had died. Her old hound dog started howling. In the next scene, Elvis and his group formed a search party. As they were walking, they heard someone yelling, "Help! Help!" in a distance. They found the old man hanging by his suspenders in a tree that was bent over a cliff. For the first time in months, Mother and I shared a genuine laugh. When I got home, Margaret looked relieved as I talked and laughed about the comical scene. The improvement was slow, but Mother was determined to see me completely well.

One day, however, we had a cruel setback. I was playing with some girls a couple houses down from our home. I swung the stick we were playing with a little harder than usual, accidentally hurting one of the girls. Her face twisted with anger and she growled, "My father said your father is dead because he was drunk and got hit by a car like a dog!" I was stunned. I felt as if my chest was going to cave in. I dropped the stick and ran home. When I got to the house, I was hysterical. I screamed, "Mommy, Pat said Daddy died drunk and got hit by a car like a dog."

My mother looked shocked and hurt. She grabbed me, embraced me, and said, "*Danis*, I know it hurts but what Pat said was just mean. I don't want you to pay attention to any negative comments about your father. Remember, Daddy really loved you."

I began to scream and cry, "Daddy! Daddy please come home."

This kind of episode became a pattern. Sometimes my mother would embrace me, other times she allowed me to release the internal pain by screaming and crying until I dropped to the floor in exhaustion. She would sit patiently and make sure I snapped out of it on my own. Many times, I saw tears in her eyes. I would get up from the floor and we would hug each other. Those tender and precious moments and my mother's persistence helped me through the rough periods. Her hard work began to pay off as I showed progress. The despondency began to subside.

It took my mother about nine months to go through the grieving process with me. One afternoon, all my siblings went to the lake. Mother and I decided to stay home. After awhile, I went to play outside. Mother came out and asked if I wanted to visit next door with her. I wanted to stay and play so she told me not to wander away. I continued making a mud cake for my doll. Suddenly, I felt a familiar presence. I stopped and looked up at the kitchen window where my father used to sit and watch me play. There he was, smiling at me. I blinked my eyes and could not believe what I was seeing. "Daddy! Daddy! You're home!" Just as I made it to the door, he became transparent and said with a smile, "*Danis*, always remember, Daddy will always love you!" A strong sensation of peace came over me. I knew I had seen my father for the last time. From that time on, the screaming and crying stopped and eventually the despondency ceased. I adapted to life without him, although I never forgot him.

The second year after his death became the hardest time in our lives. Everything began to takes its toll on my mother. My father's insurance covered his funeral expenses, but there was not much money left beyond that. Mother refused to accept the train pass she was entitled to as a benefit of my father's employment with the Canadian National Railway. She had a difficult time with widowhood. She had an income of only $139 per month to feed and cloth nine of her children. My sister, Margaret, left home to work, and my brother, George, got married. Mother barely made ends meet and, most of the time, could not provide for our basic needs.

Every now and then she would get frustrated. She would go out and get drunk as a way of relieving some of the pressure and maintaining her sanity. What was ludicrous was that she was accused of spending our money foolishly. How was it possible with the amount she was expected to live on? She was also accused of leaving us unattended, which was untrue because one of the older children was always home to care for us. Her parents and friends turned on her rather than giving her the support she needed. They betrayed her and participated in reporting her to Children's Aid. Her parents took two of their grandchildren, Vivian and Johnny, without my mother's consent. Shortly after, a social worker came to our home and took the remaining six children into custody, even though we were in the care of an older sibling of legal age.

This was something new to our family. It never happened when my parents were together. Fortunately, we were all placed together with a French family in Hearst while we remained under the guardianship of the Children's Aid. Mother attended family court. When she addressed the judge, she requested that two of her children—Theresa, a Polio victim and Michael, the baby—remain under their care for an additional nine months, explaining she could not provide for their basic needs. She requested that four of her other children be returned to her. The judge was impressed with my mother's decisions and granted her request. He commented that this was the first case he had presided involving a Native woman who expressed love for her children at the same time as showing assertiveness. We were returned to our mother with probation visits from the Children's Aid social worker. The people that reported her were surprised, because they all underestimated my mother's potential. As far as she was concerned, we were her children and no one was going to take us without a fight.

My mother was a hard-working woman. She cleaned our house, cooked whatever she could, bathed us, and washed our clothes and blankets, a task that was not bad in the summer but very difficult in the winter. She cared for us as a mother should. For a young widow, she did an exceptional job. No one bothered to assist her in other areas. Other than help getting wood ready for the winter after father died, she was on her own. Our fire would burn out during winter nights and we would wake up to a gigantic freezer. The windows would be frozen over and our canned goods would freeze and needed to be discarded, a job my mother hated because it meant less food for her children. Sometimes, she refused to get us up for school because it was too cold, a great risk because the education system was strict regarding attendance. The police made frequent visits to our home through the winter months to investigate why we were absent from school. Sometimes she kept us home because we did not have proper clothes to wear.

My brother, Fred, learned very young to become Mother's main helper. Many times, that last winter at home, I saw him cut wood and get water from the lake. He would come into the house with tears frozen to his cheeks, and the water he spilled on the way formed into ice on his pant legs. The pails he carried would be thick with ice, adding extra weight to the water inside them. He did not stop until our water container was full. When he awoke in the morning, his hard-earned water would be frozen into one big lump that bulged out of the water container.

Fred would also go to work for a few days to buy groceries. Most of the time, Mother would charge food at the general store and pay her bill at the end of each month. This repeated cycle made it virtually impossible for her to get ahead. Back then, Indian Affairs would go to all the households and distribute powdered milk and biscuits (we called them dog biscuits). Mother would boil them down and make a homemade pudding to add flavour to the tasteless biscuits. The powdered milk was a treat. That last summer, I helped my mother by picking berries so she could make jam and serve it with bannock.

It was during this time that the social worker talked my mother into placing us in the residential school in Fort Albany. I remember Mother talking to me about it. She said it would be a warm place to sleep, offer three meals a day, and look after our education and religion training. It was decided that the five of us should be sent to St. Ann's. Those of us who were old enough to understand, thought we would be cared for and our basic needs would be met. Never once did Mother mention we would be subject to any mistreatment. She did not know that some of her children would be obligated to pay a hefty price at the hands of the institution.

St. Ann's Residential School

In the fall of 1965, my mother helped us prepare to leave. She made sure we were all bathed and had a set of clean clothes to change into during our trip. That night, all our suitcases were packed and she took us to the train station the next day. She purchased tickets to Moosonee. It was a sad time for all of us. We hugged and kissed our mother as we boarded the train, one by one. When the train pulled forward, we all pressed our faces on the window so we could wave goodbye. Once Mother was no longer in sight, we settled into our seats. The younger siblings were well behaved and enjoyed the train ride.

When we arrived in Moosonee, it was late. No one greeted us, even though my father's relatives lived there. We were all tired and hungry. My brother, Fred, stopped to ask for directions to Uncle Frank's place. When we got there, Fred knocked on the door. There was no response. He stopped and said, "They must be all sleeping." We looked at each other, our eyes expressing concern for our younger siblings. In a last attempt, Fred instructed all of us to help him knock. No one came to open the door. In desperation, Fred pointed to a Bombardier in the yard. "We'll sleep in there tonight and we'll pretend we're camping," he said, and we arranged our sleeping quarters. Since it was a chilly autumn night, the ground was cold. We decided to sit up to sleep. We placed the smaller children side by side, and Fred and I, being the biggest, sat at each end. We huddled together to keep them warm with our body heat. The little ones fell asleep rather quickly, but I looked out the window directly above me and watched the diamond-studded stars twinkling in the sky. I cried silently, feeling lonely and sorry that my siblings were forced to sleep in such a deplorable place.

The next morning, the door swung open. It was Uncle Frank. He started laughing when he saw us. He said he had ignored the knocking because he thought we were drunks! He took us into the house, gave us breakfast, and got in contact with the local priest who took us to the rectory where we stayed the next night. I had a difficult time getting to sleep; there were so many changes in such a short span of time. I was on my own for the first time which made me have to come to terms with my father's death all over. The reality that he would not come and rescue us was difficult to accept. I felt powerless and insecure knowing my mother would not be able to visit because she lived so far away and did not have the means for the trip. As my tears rolled onto the starched pillowcase, I remember thinking, *"Get used to it, Mary! This is your new life."*

The next day, as Fred, Edmond, Peter, Vivian, Johnny and I stood on the dock waiting to board the plane, I noticed Vivian looking curious. Suddenly, she asked, "Where is Moosonee, then?" Edmond said, "You're standing on it!" We all started laughing. Vivian had a gift for being comical at the right time and did not know she was an inspiration to all of us.

We boarded the plane and buckled in. The pilot slammed the door and positioned the lever to lock it. It felt as if we were crammed in a little can, but my younger siblings didn't seem to mind the new transportation. The engine roared, the floaters raced down the river, splashing and throwing water up at the windows. It gradually rose into the air and I looked out the window and saw the floaters shift slowly into the compartments below the wings. After awhile, we reached a realm above the clouds. It looked as if we were floating on a bulky, dirty-grey cotton-ball blanket that was rolled out underneath us. My siblings were excited about the ride and were too young to understand what was happening.

Fred, Edmond, and I sat in silence, lost in our own thoughts. I wondered what the residential school was going to be like. How was I going to survive without seeing my mother? I kept thinking that if my father were alive, we would all be at home where we belonged. I began to feel bad for my mother because she did not have the means to care for us. My thoughts roamed to a conversation I had had with my father. I wondered if this was the heaven he had told me about. If so, would I be able to find him and get a chance to speak to him? I looked out and saw only a broad open sky.

Below us, the trees appeared flattened like a carpet of grass. The rivers looked like little veins, and the lakes, like tiny potholes. Although the flight was short, it seemed rather long. The pilot announced, through a static intercom, "We are approaching Fort Albany. Prepare for landing." I looked out the window and noticed a few buildings in the distance. I remember thinking it was odd that a big white building appeared to dominate the entire area in dense bush. As the plane descended, the floaters shifted slowly into position and landed on the river, gradually coming to a stop. Droplets from the water that had splashed up formed into big teardrops and ran across the window. I recall thinking, *"that's the way my heart aches."*

The pilot came and pulled the lever to unlock the door. He got out and grabbed a rope attached to the plane and tied it to the dock. We all got out, waited to get our luggage, and followed Fred. My younger siblings stayed around me as they usually did when feeling shy or uncomfortable.

A nun instructed us to follow her. I inspected the strange surroundings and concluded we had been let off in the bush in the middle of nowhere. I noticed one dirt road which led to the mission or to the village. I took a deep breath and slowly exhaled, tired from the adventures since I left home. It felt good to have my feet on the ground and to feel the sun shine on me. Our guide led us to a landing. The buildings I had glimpsed from the air came into clear view. There was a hospital, nurse's residence, rectory, and a barn. As we continued, we came to a culvert, and I noticed a wooden bridge on the other side. Below, was the sound of the stream running through the property.

In the distance, stood a big, white, brick building with numerous windows and steel staircases which seemed to dominate the area. I was stunned because the building looked just like the jail my grandparents had taken me to to visit my Uncle Ron. Another lady, dressed in black, yelled from the balcony, "Welcome to St. Ann's. Where do you come from?"

Fred replied, "Hearst."

"What grade are you in?"

"Grade eight," he answered.

"So you will be with me?"

"I guess so."

"Okay! I'll see you later," she replied. With that, she turned and walked back into the building.

The nun that we were with led us to a side door. Once inside, I had to give my eyes a chance to adjust after the blinding sun. The lights were dim but seemed to reflect on the shiny floor. Suddenly, the big door slammed shut behind us with a loud bang. We were startled and responded by laughing nervously. Fred and the nun continued speaking quietly. During the conversation, he glanced over my way, looking deeply concerned. Something was wrong. We continued waiting and standing in the hallway. A sudden chill sent a shiver down my spine. I looked at my siblings who did not appear to have noticed it. I shook it off but it bothered me.

Shortly after, another nun came and greeted us. Without warning, she said, "Okay, girls follow me! Boys follow her!" We were stunned. My little brother, Johnny, started crying because he wanted to be with me. I wanted to console him but instinct told me it would be unwise. As we parted, my brother's cries echoed down the halls. The hardest thing I had to do was ignore him, and I remember thinking, *"No one told me it was going to be like this."*

The only comfort I knew was that my little sister, Vivian, would be with me. I took her hand and continued walking, gradually swallowing the lump in my throat.

Becoming a Member of the Group

The nun we followed was Sister Deanna. She was an Ojibway Native from an isolated Native community. Her attire made her look tall and her shoulders broad. A sheer black veil decorated the white headpiece that covered her hair, and the white background brought out her dark complexion. What was most noticeable was her high forehead with a deep wrinkle stretching downward. Later, I learned Sister Deanna would be the supervisor assigned to us for the school year. She was not as friendly as she appeared when the other nun was present and did not bother to speak with us, so we all walked in silence.

Suddenly, she stopped and opened a door to a room filled with little Native girls all dressed the same. I thought they were identical! She instructed us to give her our luggage and to wait while she went to another room. A short while later, she came out with housecoats, towels, and toiletry items. She continued to walk and led us into a musty smelling basement where we were told to get undressed and change into a garment that looked like a full-sized apron. She broke the silence by saying we were to wear this garment every time we showered, so we did not expose our bodies and commit sin.

Sister Deanna approached me and applied a strong-smelling liquid to my hair. My eyes stung, my nostrils felt like they were on fire, and my skin felt like it was burning. I stood waiting while Vivian got the same treatment. She began to whimper, so I felt for her hand to assure her I was nearby. Next, Sister Deanna instructed us to get into a large room that had pipes running along the ceiling. I almost panicked because it reminded me of a movie I had seen back home in which people entered a similar room and died. I was relieved to discover it was a shower. When we were finished, Sister Deanna gave us robes to wear. She picked up our clothes and we followed her into a dormitory. The beds were very neatly made, all in a row, with towels hung evenly at the head of each. Our beds were on the third row.

Vivian and I watched as Sister Deanna took our clothes and stuffed them inside our suitcase. She took Vivian's teddy bear and forced it in the case. All she said, as she took our suitcase to a closet and locked it away, was, "You won't be needing these." She proceeded to another closet, and said, "Names are not used here, only numbers. You are number thirty-two. Whenever you hear the number, you are to step forward." I must have looked confused because she asked, "Do you understand?"

"Yeah," I replied.

She looked at me and said, "From now on, you are to answer, 'Yes, Sister Deanna.'"

I responded with a question: "Yes, Sister Deanna?" She looked at me and it made me feel nervous. She turned back to the closet and handed me a jumper, white blouse, sweater, undergarments, stockings, and garters. As I was dressing, I could not help but notice a "thirty-two" marked inside my clothes. I did not know how to wear garters, so Sister Deanna used Vivian as a model to show me. I felt embarrassed. Sister Deanna grabbed a black pair of shoes from the shelf and threw them at my feet, saying in a rough voice, "Put them on."

After getting dressed, we followed her back to the recreation room. Sister Deanna went into her office. When she came out, she took a chair and ordered me to sit down. I obeyed and watched my hair fall to the floor as she began cutting. The other girls stood around me and smiled. When I was done, I looked just like the other girls with a Robin Hood hairstyle. Vivian followed and looked uncomfortable. I sensed her insecurity so I stood where she could see me. I smiled at her and she seemed to calm down and look more confident.

When she was done, I took her hand and led her to some chairs nearby. I tried talking to the other girls, but they only smiled or giggled without answering me. Later that day, I learned that out of thirty-four girls, the majority spoke Cree, some spoke Ojibway, others spoke Oji-Cree and only five of us spoke fluent English. No one was punished for speaking their mother tongue, however, language was a barrier that caused problems for most of us.

On that first day, I noticed the other girls were playing, talking, and laughing. I was amazed at the alertness they were trained to have without communication. Sister Deanna clapped her hands twice, and the girls became silent, stood side by side, and formed two lines according to our number system. Sister Deanna waited for a few seconds until everyone was calm. She opened the door, clapped her hands once, and the girls followed her out. Like little soldiers, we marched to the cafeteria and stood by the benches. The only time the girls spoke was to pray before the meal. When they finished eating, Sister Deanna went to the younger group and led them to the door. We followed and returned to the recreation room.

At first, I thought I was imagining things. It was revealed to me that the girls were trained to listen and go by sound. While the girls were playing, Sister Deanna clapped her hands twice. The girls responded by silence and formed two lines. She opened the door and the girls followed her into the dorm across the hall. Everyone walked in silence and stopped by their beds. Sister Deanna broke the silence as she led us into prayer. When we were done, we prepared for bed. I looked over at my sister who seemed unsure of herself. I smiled at her and gave a little wave. Sister Deanna glared at me. I sensed the gesture was unacceptable and it would not be wise to do it again.

That first night in bed, I realized my individuality had been taken from me. My name was replaced with a number. My personal clothing was replaced with a uniform. My siblings were exchanged for a group of strange girls. My home was replaced by this strict setting. A cold nun replaced my mother's loving warmth. I had lost my freedom to a controlled environment. I broke down and allowed myself to cry. In a matter of minutes, the sounds of sniffles filled the dorm. It became our place of refuge, a private ritual we all practiced on a nightly basis.

I learned the schedule from the girls. Every morning, Sister Deanna woke us up with a manual school bell. We got on our knees to pray. Then we would line up to go to the bathroom, wash up, brush our teeth, and dress. We made up our beds very tightly, placed folded pajamas under the pillow, and hung our towels and facecloths evenly at the head of the bed frame. When we were finished, we had to wait for the little girls and were not allowed to help them. Sister Deanna was good at supervising by pacing back and forth, watching us. Once everyone was done, we proceeded to the cafeteria where we prayed, sat, and ate our breakfasts. Then we returned to the recreation room. A majority of the girls waited for classes. Janet, Doreen, and I had chores to do before class.

We were not allowed to roam around the school. Sister Deanna would escort us to our chores in the dormitory across the hall. I was assigned to wash the toilets in the stalls, Janet swept and mopped the floor, and Doreen washed the sinks. The rule of silence was enforced the entire time. After chores, Sister Deanna would come for us, and we would join the lineup to our classes.

Double Messages

Surprisingly, we were allowed to be in class with boys. In the first year, I was taught by Sister Bennett. She was non-Native, French, and overweight, and her habit made her look bigger. Our day went according to her mood swings. We were taught basic reading, writing, arithmetic, a touch of geography, history, and art on Fridays. Catechism was emphasized and instructed by Father Andrews.

Some days, I enjoyed class time; on other days, I dreaded being there. Competition became a crucial part of our learning. Once a month, Sister Bennett called out our names, starting with those who achieved the highest marks and ending with the lowest. I usually came in third and I remained there for the rest of the term. My heart always went out to two peers. Don was a resident of the school and Frank was from the village. They were always singled out by Sister Bennett and ridiculed by the pets and bullies of our class.

Don was very shy and very closed. He had a hard time with his studies which I blamed on the language. I was rather disappointed that our teacher did not pick up on that. Instead, he was constantly criticized in class. He was called "lazy," "stupid," "good for nothing," a person who would "amount to nothing but a bum." The classroom bullies would laugh at him. So many times, I watched and hurt for him. Gradually, without the proper support, Don lost interest in learning. One day, we heard someone snoring. Everyone was suddenly wide awake and we looked around. Sister Bennett began to walk up and down the aisles. She stopped right beside Don and slammed her hand down on his desk, making a loud sound. Don jumped. He had fallen asleep with his eyes opened. Once again, the pets and bullies laughed at him, including our teacher.

Frank was friendly. He had a weight problem, possibly because he was big-boned. He also had an acne problems, poor hygiene, and always wore his cleanest dirty clothes. This was undoubtedly due to improper facilities at his home. The pets and bullies always made fun of him. They called him, "fat ass," "pus face," and "stink skunk" in the Cree language. One morning, after prayer, Sister Bennett asked one of her pets to translate what the other students were saying to Frank. At first, I thought she was going to correct them. Instead, she grinned and laughed along with them. I looked at Frank, who was deeply upset and hurt. He too began to lose interest in learning, missed school frequently, and finally dropped out.

The bullies did not like me much for not participating in making fun of and laughing at Don and Frank. I was teased and called *Whoo-mei-soo*, meaning "owl," because I had round eyes. Some days were really bad. I used to look forward to recess.

Most of the time, recess involved walking in a circle. Our classroom had two doors. We walked out one door into the hall and then into the other door through the class. This was repeated until recess was over. The odd time, we were permitted to go back to our recreation room for "*collation* time" which, in French, means "snack time." We would be served broken cookies the staff did not want.

One day, I was having a hard time. I could not understand fractions. I wrote a note to my friend, Cecil, that said, "I can't understand this. Will you help me later?" Sister Bennett caught Cecil trying to hide the note. She put her hand out, motioning to Cecil to hand it over. Reluctantly, Cecil gave it to her. Sister Bennett took it as an insult. She ordered me to stand up. She began to criticize and mock me, and I started crying. The class roared with laughter while Cecil looked upset and sorry I was put in such an embarrassing position. Finally, Sister Bennett ordered me to sit down and began to explain the arithmetic process. I was too upset to understand. Through every subject thereafter, Sister Bennett would say, "Now, let's look at what you may not understand...." All that day, I kept my head down. Shame can do a lot to a child.

In December that year, all classes participated in a Christmas composition contest. When I entered the school, I understood that Jesus had been born in a stable. Sister Bennett looked over my contest submission and made some changes to my story. Two weeks later, Sister Superior read a winning composition over the intercom. She requested the winner come forward because there was no name on it. I looked around and was surprised when Sister Bennett told me to go to the office to pick up my prize! On the way to the office, I kept wondering whether Jesus was born in the stable or in the middle of the ocean.

I won a doll and did not feel good about it. I accepted the prize with a plastic smile, feeling I had participated in lying, stealing, and cheating. I felt guilty, knowing the contest was fixed. That night, I noticed a sting on the doll's head, so I pulled it through the loop on my bed frame. When I went to bed that night, the doll went missing. Sister Deanna glanced at me with a smirk on her face. I remember thinking, "Did she have to steal it? All she had to do was ask for it!" For the longest time, I wondered if I should confess my sins because I took part in dishonesty. Would Sister Bennett and Sister Superior confess? How about Sister Deanna for stealing my doll? Sin was never mentioned in relation to them.

In class, students did not have to be gifted or talented, just liked. For example, during public speaking, I was the first to go up in front of the class because I did not show my shyness and spoke good English. But that did not necessarily mean I would win. Many of my classmates' presentations were far better than those of the two pets Sister Bennett selected.

The nuns involved in my life had double standards. I was too young to understand and was afraid to ask why there was no wrong in what they did. Even Father Andrews lived the opposite of what he taught. He would have us recite prayers. We would go through our Catechism book. The message that stayed with me was to love everyone. A few days later, Father Andrews would come in with a manual projector and set up a Bambo film. He would read out what Bambo was praying in church: "God, forgive the savages for practicing witchcraft for the heathens do not know what they do." Father Andrews convinced us that if we refused to obey Bambo, we would all go to hell! He taught us that the Roman Catholic Church was the only denomination through which we would make it to heaven; the other denominations were going to hell and eternal fire!

The Annual Visits

In the two years I stayed at St. Ann's, preparing for annual visits from government officials was a crucial time. Our routine was changed, rigid rules were elevated, our daily uniforms altered to formal attire, our meals upgraded. All staff showered us with temporary love which was strange compared to the usual coldness we endured. We staged talent shows to entertain and impress the officials. A festive scene hid the silent cries of Native children and youth in despair.

In the first visit, all the girls wore red jumpers with white blouses. All the boys wore light blue shirts, navy blazers, and grey trousers. In the second visit, the colours were altered. All the girls wore burgundy jumpers with white blouses. All the boys wore white shirts, navy blazers and grey trousers. The formal wear worn by the girls was strictly for these special visits. On Sundays, we wore sailor outfits and daily we wore ordinary plaid jumpers. The boys wore their best uniforms on special visits and

Sundays. The rest of the time, they wore plain attire that resembled prison shirts with navy pants.

Before the arrival of the government officials, a red carpet strip was rolled out, leading up to the metal stairway. All the groups—boys and girls—met in front of the school. When the officials arrived, we would greet them by singing St. Ann's theme as they walked on the red carpet. Then we would wait for half an hour outside the school while they inspected it. This did not take too long because all students participated in cleaning; our supervisors, teachers, and the other staff made sure everything was spotless and orderly.

Afterwards, we would return to our designated recreation rooms. Then we would meet in the cafeteria. On these visits, our menu changed. We were served turkey, mashed potatoes, gravy, and vegetables, with ice cream for desert. The sliding doors that usually separated boys and girls were opened for us to eat together. The rule of silence was temporarily banned and we were allowed to talk as we ate.

Later, all the groups met downstairs. Once again, the sliding doors that separated the boys and girls were opened. Chairs were set up for our guests. Our president always presented and delivered a report about how our supervisors provided excellent care for us. In closing, he would stress how the students appreciated the school. The students would then put on a dynamic talent show, something we practiced for weeks to impress the government officials. Everything the president mentioned was very convincing and we confirmed it by participating and staging a scene for the entire evening. Younger boys and girls sang songs. Older boys demonstrated Boy Scout skills. Older girls demonstrated Girl Guide and cheer-leading skills. Our school band members played their instruments beautifully because they were bribed with money to pay attention to the nun who conducted us. Winners of speaking contests presented their topics. The students and staff would fill the room with smiles and laughter. By the time we completed our "show boating," the government officials left with the image that we were one big happy family living in an institution they funded. Sadly, some of us secretly contributed the tips and bonuses to gratify priests, nuns, and lay people.

The next day, after the officials left, we returned to a regular routine, ordinary uniforms, basic menu, and the regime lifestyle we were conditioned to follow. Names were omitted. The only places we were addressed by name were classrooms and at special public events. Family relationships were discouraged even though many of us had brothers and sisters in attendance. The school was infested with violations; children were subject to physical, mental, emotional, verbal, sexual and spiritual abuse. We lived in a military setting. Failure to comply resulted in severe corporal punishment behind closed doors. Enforced assimilation was applied by keeping us away from our families and communities, taking our individuality, locking away our personal items, and separating us from our siblings. Religion was forced as all students were required to make Confirmation or Communion by a certain age. There was no privacy; even our mail was tampered with. Parcels were opened and inspected and, once opened, kept in the office. Students had to ask permission for access to them. Letters that were written by students were censored before they could be sealed and mailed. Normal needs were not met. Older girls that had reached menstruation were denied access to sanitary napkins which were locked away in the office. These girls were forced to ask for one whenever a change was required. Even the designated playground was controlled and segregated into four areas. In the front of the school, little boys and big boys shared half of the playground. At the back of the school was a portable for the older girls' dormitory. A chain-link fence marked the area off limits. On the other side, was the bigger girls' playground, the far end of which was established by an invisible marking which the little girls were trained not to cross.

Even in a place with so much dysfunction, there was a balance of good experiences. We shared rare times as a group of people and were briefly released from the rigid policies of the school. Once in a while, we were treated to movies: *"The Butterfly Catcher," "Seven Brides for Seven Brothers," "The Ten Commandments," "Gone with the Wind,"* and *"Shenandoah."* Other times, we assembled and enjoyed presentations made by other students. Once, for example, the students went for a school trip. Laughs roared when the speaker, Edmond Sackaney, told of his comical adventures. We were sometimes invited to watch a variety show the older students put together to entertain us. These were times we shared not as staff and students, but as human beings.

For outdoor activities, I recall standing in front of the school with other students and staff. We all participated in the Winter Carnival. I remember seeing the coronation of our queen, a gorgeous girl named Rita. She looked more Metis than Native, and I thought her beauty looked out of place. Nevertheless, she was a St. Ann's resident student who came from Winisk (now Peawanuck). As the queen was announced, I remember seeing Bonhomie Carnival get all excited. He approached her to put his arm around her neck. Instead, he accidentally hit her head and almost knocked her crown off. Queen Rita got upset and yelled, "Take it easy!" We all started laughing. Bonhomie Carnival was a young teacher who had a crush on Rita. That day, there were all kinds of activities for all ages to enjoy, including a fish-pond booth that was set up for the younger children. The cheering and laughing echoed from every direction.

Many of the changes that took place had to do with Sister Superior. Whether educational or inspirational, she made an effort to direct us properly. I recall Sister Superior interrupting class to allow us to listen to international news over the intercom. Once, we heard the blast off of man going to the moon. She made it exciting. Another time, we heard reports of the assassination of John F. Kennedy. Even though we did not know him, we were requested to show respect by standing for three minutes of silence when he was pronounced dead.

While I was at St. Ann's, Sister Superior was placed in the sad position of having to announce deaths. The first was the death of young Brother Landers. He was popular and loved by all the students. For some reason, he became sick and we later heard he had died of cancer. The second death was of a student named Andy who had been practicing for St. Ann's last track and field event. I remember looking out the window and watching him do a relay. He was running so fast, he impressed me. Then I saw him drop to the ground. I thought he had hurt his ankle and could not get up. Suddenly, some staff members came running with a stretcher. They put Andy on it and carried him away. Shortly after, Sister Superior announced that Andy had died of heart failure. Both times, we bowed our heads in a three-minute silence to show respect for two young men that touched our lives and crossed our paths.

Sister Superior also made appointments to meet with different groups for pep talks. I saw her grouchy a few times, but what impressed me was the way she handled us. If we were all talking, she would fold her arms and pace back and forth until we responded with silence. Then she would say, "thank you," and proceed to correct us, always with sensitivity. No matter what, she would end with a joke. Never once did she raise her hand or voice to us. Her way was productive because we responded by making an effort to change and improve.

In my second year, Sister Superior arranged a floor-hockey competition between staff and older boys and girls. We all cheered and laughed when each side scored. It was funny watching the nuns trip on their dresses, veils flying in every direction. That same evening, we had our first dance. Everyone laughed because no one was dancing, so Sister Superior got a group of us up and made us start the dance. Then the nuns and staff sat back and laughed at us. We laughed together and no student was ridiculed.

On occasion, Sister Superior authorized leave from the school for weekends of camping. Sister Rita would make arrangements with the kitchen staff to prepare and pack our food. There was a side of Sister Rita's character that she did not show too often. She was fun to be with. Once we arrived at the girls' camp, she would ask the younger girls to gather kindling for our stove. In the meantime, she and the older girls would put the food away and set up. Whatever we ate tasted good because of the team effort put into it.

Sister Rita spent quality time with us. She would participate in hide and seek, tag, and roam with us in the bushes. Before dark, we would gather the kindling and make a bonfire to roast our wieners and marshmallows. When we went inside, Sister Rita would make a fresh pot of tea and give us big pieces of homemade bread, spread margarine and jam, which we dunked in the tea.

As we all settled in for the night, we would laugh as we tried to smooth our straw mattresses. Then we would literally "hit the hay," with our clothes on. We fell asleep to the sound of the stove crackling, and some of us lay on our top bunks and stared at the star-filled sky.

For a couple of days, we took advantage of being away from the pressures of school. We participated in all activities as friends. When we went back to the school, we separated into two classes: supervisors and students.

Sister Superior and Sister Rita allowed the staff to be involved with our lives. Some staff members would come and teach us different skills or just spend time with us. It was always a refreshing change. For example, Ms. St. Denis use to gather all the groups and show us slides of pictures she took around the school. She was our own personal photographer. One Sunday afternoon, she took the older girls group for a walk to our campsite. Once we got there, we all gathered kindling and made a fire. Ms. Ste Denis found an old pot and melted margarine and marshmallows, which she mixed with Special K since we didn't have Rice Krispies. When it was ready, she broke it into chunks and passed it around. I remember the girls joking and calling her "ka-shuk" because she served herself a big piece. Ms. St. Denis knew they were saying something, so she asked for an interpretation. The girls laughed and said, "you're greedy!" She laughed right along with us. Although these were rare times, it helped me through my hardest moments. I kept the memories alive and close to my heart.

Then there were the secrets which some have chosen to conceal. Some of these secrets remain blocked out, kept by the walls of St. Ann's. Some of their keepers have died prematurely of alcohol and/or drug abuse or suicide and taken the secrets with them. Others just got old and chose not to remember the past. Some, like me, have decided to heal by disclosing the love/hate relationships that have affected us for two or three generations.

Secrets Within the Group

Sister Deanna always had ways of enforcing compliance. There were abuses of all kinds and I quickly learned that one could be traumatized whether or not she was directly involved. Sister Deanna committed these acts in two ways: what I experienced with the group and what I experienced as an individual.

Our basic right to go to the bathroom was denied. Instead, we were trained to control our bladders and bowels. We were allowed to go only when Sister Deanna escorted us as a group. We took turns using the bathroom and waited in line for the others to finish. Then we were escorted back to the recreation room.

Our shower time could be enjoyable or it could be a torture chamber. We all wore shower garments to cover our bodies. Sister Deanna would wait for us to shampoo our hair. Suddenly, when we least expected it, she would turn the cold water on full blast. She would be prepared at the entrance, wearing a rubber apron and rubber boots.

As the girls attempted to escape the cold water, Sister Deanna would shove, push, and punch them back in. The excessive force caused girls to fall on their bottoms directly under the cold water. The shower room would be filled with cries from shampoo stinging our eyes, pain from a punch or fall, all combined from the shock of cold water. When it was over, our bodies literally shook, our teeth chattered, our skin was covered with goosebumps. The only explanation Sister Deanna gave us, with a grin on her face, was, "It's good for you." After numerous such episodes, I became an expert at standing on my toes against the wall to avoid the cold water.

When Sister Deanna wanted peace and quiet, she gained it using two methods. First she would make us stand in silence like statues in front of our chairs. She would sit in her office and check on us by glancing through her big glass window. When she noticed the smaller girls becoming restless, she would come out of her office. The delightful smiles on the little girls' faces would turn into frowns. Then she would order us to sit and remain in silence. Later, I would admire the small girls because they made it through the unnecessary ordeal for up to five hours! The second method Sister Deanna used, was placing us outdoors which was not bad if it was warm but very unwise when it was cold. We were not adequately dressed for the frigid temperature. The gusty winds were so strong they blew snow across the open field. At first, we jumped around to keep warm. The little girls would cry and their teardrops would freeze to their cheeks. Our eyes would be watery from the coldness. After a few experiences of this ordeal, the other four older girls and I got smart. We took charge of the younger and smaller girls. We would instruct them to race for the industrial dryer vent underneath the metal staircase. We would form a circle and place the smaller girls in the center to keep them warm with our body heat and protect them from the wind. Many times, Sister Deanna greeted us at the door with a grin on her face and her famous explanation: "It's good for you."

Every now and then, Sister Deanna's violent outbursts escalated into beatings. A girl could be hit for losing a personal item, for looking at Sister Deanna the wrong way, for attempting to explain herself, for breaking the rule of silence, for bedwetting. Sister Deanna justified her actions by her responsibility for teaching us. In reality, it was to keep us under control. Whenever a girl was being beaten, we were forced to watch without flinching or showing emotion. I watched girls slapped across the face repeatedly until their cheeks were red, hair pulled and heads yanked in every direction, heads banged on hard surfaces, hair grabbed at the back, above the hairline, to suspend the girl in the air, girls lifted off their feet by their wrists. Girls were struck with excessive force with an open hand, backhand, or fist, causing nosebleeds or lacerations to the mouth and lip area. Girls were shoved, pushed, thrown around the room or to the floor. Girls were punched, kicked, and bruised in unnoticeable areas such as the stomach, back, arms, legs. A rule we all followed was never to discuss it. My own beatings were severe. After awhile, I convinced myself it was normal and Sister Deanna did it for my own good.

Once, when the other girls and I were getting dressed to go outside, I realized I had lost my moccasin. Sister Deanna became upset and was very angry by the time she found it. She hit and beat me with it. She slapped my face and repeatedly hit me over the head until I was crouched on the floor. I tried to protect myself by using my arms to shield the blows. It was useless. Finally, as I staggered to my feet, I was crying. Sister Deanna screamed, "Next time, don't lose it."

Another time, while playing, I accidentally hit Tammy with my arm as it swung out. I stopped when I realized what had happened and checked to make sure she was okay. I apologized to her and resumed playing. Without any warning, Sister Deanna grabbed me by the back of the collar and twirled me around. She started slapping me in the face, continued by grabbing my hair and yanking my head at the same time. I was so shocked I didn't know how to react. I began to cry even though she told me not to. She became so angry, she slapped me with a backhand, hitting my nose and mouth area. The taste of blood filled my mouth, which I was forced to swallow. When it was over, I was trembling. Sister Deanna said, "Next time, pick on someone your size!"

My thoughts escaped my lips. "You're bigger than me. Why is it okay for you?"

She slapped me across the face and yelled, "Don't answer back and don't look at me that way!" The tears that ran down my cheeks felt as if they burned my skin. My head hurt from the lumps that had formed.

Another incident occurred in the dormitory where Cecil, Janet, and I did our chores. Everything started out normal. My chore was to wash toilets. That morning, I avoided washing the first bathroom stall because someone had had diarrhea and had not flushed it. I decided to start at the end and work my way up. Finally, as I was about to enter the first stall, I was distracted by sounds from Cecil and Janet. They were talking and laughing. I decided there was no harm in checking out what was so funny. The girls had braided their dirty industrial mops and were dancing with them. I watched for a while and started laughing. As I turned away to finish washing the first stall, someone grabbed me by the back of my collar and yanked me so roughly, I heard a rip. I was twirled around and there was Sister Deanna. She began to slap my face repeatedly. I started crying and my tears stung my cheeks. Grabbing my hair, she started yanking my head in every direction. She got ahold of my hair at the back of my head, forcing me into a bent position. All I was able to do was follow as I was forcibly led into the stall that I had not finished cleaning. She proceeded to bang my head back and forth between the walls of the cubical. She forced me to my knees and shoved my face in the toilet bowl containing the diarrhea. I started gagging. She held onto my hair and pulled my head back to a tilt and made me swallow. This was repeated three times. My hair, face, and mouth tasted and smelled like human waste. When it was over, my entire body shook. I was nauseated. Sister Deanna screamed, "The next time you will be obedient and work in silence!" She ordered me to wash up. I regurgitated. Cecil, Janet, and I never said anything about what happened. We knew it would be safer not to.

When I went to class, Sister Bennett asked, "Who smells like...?" Before she finished, I put my hand up. She ordered me to the front. I walk forward with my head down. She escorted me out of the class and took me to the teacher's lounge where she asked, very gently, "What happened?"

I avoided eye contact for the fear of crying and because my eyes were already puffy. I replied in a very low voice, "Washing the bathroom." We stood silence. She knew I was already upset, so she reached for a shelf and handed me some Jergens hand lotion which I gladly used. Sister Bennett looked at me concerned, sensing I was not going to say any more.

That night, as I lay on my bed, my body ached from head to toe. My hair was stiff and smelled like feces. As tears rolled down my face, the scenes of the incident flashed before me. I could not believe it happened or understand why Sister Deanna went to such drastic measures. Drifting into sleep, the last question that came to mind was, *"Is this why Indians are brown?"* I ate and slept in that state for a full week. For the longest time, I scrubbed my face until the soap stripped and chapped my skin. I brushed my teeth until my gums bled.

The very last beating took place in the recreation room. I was wrongfully accused of stealing candy from one of the girls. Sometimes, other girls would implicate someone else to avoid a run-in with Sister Deanna. I tried to explain that I did not steal any candy but was nervous and became intimidated when she stood there and stared at me. I gave her the impression I was guilty, and she slapped me across the face, grabbed my hair, and yanked my head. When she let go of me, I fell on to the floor and then got up to go to my chair. Sister Deanna pushed me from behind; I lost my balance, fell on my knees, and slid across the floor, crashing between two chairs which caused my head to hit the radiator. My head hurt so much, I touched my forehead and noticed blood on my hand. It seeped down into my eye. I panicked and let out a scream but stopped when Sister Deanna said, "Don't cry, and don't scream!" She helped me up by grabbing the top of my hair. My knees buckled and I slumped to the floor. I felt a kick in my stomach, gasped for air and held my belly, rolling from side to side. I noticed her foot raised and tried to avoid it but was too slow. She got me in the spine.

By this time, she seemed more upset. I can remember screaming in my mind, *"Someone, please help me! Please stop. I'll be good. Oh! God help me...."* Nothing was coming out of my mouth. Sister Deanna instructed me to get up. I staggered to my feet and slumped back to the floor. I was exhausted and heard ringing in my left ear. Everything sounded as if I was under water. Sudden rage rose in me when I saw my lifeless hair smeared with blood on the floor. Once again, I screamed in my head, *"Why don't you just kill me and get it over with! If I had a knife, I would kill you! I hate your guts! I wish I were dead!"* All of a sudden, I had a vision of a little girl. She was bruised, alone, and crying. In my mind, I let out a little smile, picked her up, and put her in a rosebud.

Sister Deanna brought me back to reality by grabbing the back of my hair. As I stood, my legs felt numb. I attempted to take a step forward, only to fall on the floor again. At this point, I stopped crying and said to myself, *"Come on Mary, stand up and walk!"* Sister Deanna demanded I go to the dormitory and wash up. Amazingly, my legs responded. She followed me and rambled on about obedience. I drowned her out by withdrawing into myself. It was the only way I knew to escape. That night, my entire body throbbed from the pain.

Things did settle down afterward. I became like a robot and complied with everything. The fear Sister

Deanna instilled in me that day imprisoned my emotions.

Not long after, it was time for Confirmation. Sister Deanna informed me she was going to get the outfits for Vivian and me. I made an effort to her I had already been confirmed before I entered the school. I failed to convince her. To avoid a confrontation, I backed down because I knew what she was capable of doing. However, I was not keen on the idea of meeting with Father Andrews prior to my Confirmation.

Father Andrew was the priest who made frequent visits to our recreation room. He would sit on a chair, put his robe to the side, place little girls between his legs, and caress their bodies. If he had a little girl on his lap, he would move her to rub against him. Sister Deanna never said a word; she would just watch. I sensed there was something wrong in how he treated the little girls, so I stayed away from him and did not permit my sister Vivian to be near him.

A few days later, I was sent to Father Andrews unsupervised. He asked me questions about what I had learned in Catechism. Every time I got a right answer, he kissed me. This proceeded until his sloppy tongue slid across my neck. I was scared and uncomfortable and his breath smelled bad. The sight of his loose priest collar made me sick. The whiskers on his wrinkled face burned my skin. At the same time, he rubbed his hands all over my body. I froze when his hand slipped into my underwear. I panicked and let out a muffled scream. I felt sweat forming on my face and became nauseated. He let go of me and his breathing was rapid. He said that it would not have happened if I had not tempted him and that I had to ask God to forgive me because I committed sin and caused him to sin. I was confused. I did not know what to think. Then he said not to tell anyone and concluded by saying, "You're not only ready for Confirmation but also Communion!" As I left the room, I was dizzy and disoriented. After a few minutes of wandering down the hall, I realized I was going in the wrong direction. I stopped and leaned against the wall and could not comprehend what had just happened. I felt dirty, ashamed, and numb and stopped by the dormitory with my hand over my mouth. I ran into the cubical and vomited. When I returned to the recreation room, I felt paranoid, nervous, and sick.

For several days, I thought I was invisible. I convinced myself no one could see me. I became very quiet and withdrawn. Sister Deanna noticed, but she did not handle me in a sensitive manner. She was passing out dresses and stared at me. I sensed somehow I had become visible. She centered me out in front of all the girls by throwing the fancy dress she had in her hands at me and saying, "Here, take this fancy dress. You want attention, anyway. Maybe this will put a smile on your face." Except for a few, the girls started laughing. She embarrassed me but I did not show it.

That week, I tried desperately to come out of my shell. One morning, I decided a change of hairstyle might make me feel better. I took my comb and carefully combed my hair to the side. When I was done, I got into line as we proceeded to walk forward. Sister Deanna yanked me out of the line, shook me up, slapped me across the face, grabbed my hair and messed it up. She growled, "What is wrong with you?" I responded by looking her in the eyes and showing no emotion. She looked surprised that I did not cry. Sister Deanna left me alone for the remainder of the year. The beatings continued for some girls until they, too, stopped crying.

Summer Break

We were all excited as the summer holidays rolled around. We put all the differences aside and forget the experiences we had endured. It was like nothing happened. After ten months at St. Ann's, my siblings and I were on our way home.

When we finally got home, we were so happy to see our mother! After had been there for only two days, Ms. St. Denis made a surprise visit. She informed my mother that we had been selected from St. Ann's to attend Expo '67 in Montreal, Quebec. It took her awhile to convince Mother to allow us to go, not only because it meant our holidays with her were over, but also because her children would not be living together. Vivian and I would stay with Ms. St. Denis, while Edmond, Peter, and John would be with Mr. Mc Bain, a supervisor from the school who resided in Hull. Mother reluctantly allowed us to go as it was a once-in-a-lifetime opportunity, all expenses paid by the federal government. She kissed and hugged us with sadness in her eyes. When we got into the taxi, we waved until we could no longer see her.

When we got to Hearst, we boarded a train bound for North Bay and transferred to another headed for Ottawa. I was sad, but the ride was enjoyable. Prior to our transfer, we waited at the train station in North Bay. Ms. St. Denis allowed my brothers to walk around and instructed them not to wander away. She came and sat with Vivian and me. An intoxicated man sat across from us and unintentionally entertained us. He was fighting sleep. His head would slowly slump forward, then move to the right, tilt back, roll to the left, and quickly swing upright to its normal position. He would sit straight for a few seconds. All of a sudden, his head would slump forward and repeat the same cycle. Vivian and I looked at each other and started giggling uncontrollably. Ms. St. Denis noticed we were giggling because our bodies were shaking from silent laughter. She tried to stop us but eventually gave in and joined the laughter. It was an icebreaker for the three of us—a new beginning for our friendship.

When we arrived in Ottawa, Mr. Mc Bain came to pick up my brothers. I felt like crying because I really wanted to be with them. Sadly, they went one way and we went the other. We stayed with Ms. St. Denis's sister in Ottawa that night. For the first time that evening, I realized I felt close to a person outside my family. The next day, we left for Ms. St. Denis' family farm in the outskirts of Ottawa—a town called Plantagnet. As we traveled down the highway, we turned onto a concession road. The trees added beauty to the fair-sized farm that came into view. They had cows, pigs, chickens, and a bull, as well as a dog that helped gather the cows in the fields and guide them home. They had a huge cornfield, another garden for vegetables, and a spacious yard where Vivian and I would play.

Her family welcomed us and treated us as integral members. A single person, Ms. St. Denis took excellent care of us that summer. We were well fed and always clean. She and her mother were very sensitive to our feelings. Whenever we got lonely, she would embrace us and say, "When we go shopping, we will get a little gift for your mother. I'll take some pictures of you both and you can help prepare the parcel, okay?" Vivian and I would be so happy. They seemed to sense when the worst part of our homesickness was over. They always shared quality time and kept us busy. Her mother was a very caring and hard-working person who supported her daughter when it came to us. She was really skillful at sewing and made matching skirts for us, using mint green material to which she added red Expo logos. Very unique and eye-catching!

Her youngest brother, Allen, did not speak much English, but he used to enjoy wrestling with me, not in front of his sister but in the privacy of our rink in the cornfield. We use to really rough each other up and laugh the entire time. When we got home, we acted and looked innocent. I think Ms. St. Denis knew something was going on. She would observe our sheepish grins but never questioned us because she liked the interaction. Once in awhile, Allen would show off. He would take a baseball bat and hit one of the pigs in the behind. He was a mischievous but comical guy. We had a lot of fun with him.

The other family member Vivian and I liked playing with was Jack, the police officer. He was married to one of Ms. St. Denis' sisters. One afternoon, it was really hot. Ms. St. Denis got out the portable plastic swimming pool she had bought as a surprise for us and changed us into bathing suits. It was such a relief! Jack stopped by for a visit, and I jumped out and started running. He came running after me. I made a sharp turn and saw the swimming pool, but it was too late to stop. I slipped right in, making a big splash. We all laughed. Sometimes, when Jack ran after us, he would catch us and lift us into the air. He was a very nice man with a lovable character.

Finally, Vivian, Ms. St. Denis, and I went to Expo. People from different nationalities proudly displayed their pavilions. Ms. St. Denis kept our passport books which were stamped at every location we visited. We got on a ride which was set up like a safari and saw animals from every country. We saw people perform in talent shows. I remember watching the demonstration of a man who had trained a dolphin to jump through hoops, dance for a few seconds as it came up from under water, and make sounds like the song "Happy Birthday." As a reward, the trainer would give the dolphin a fish. Later that day, Vivian and I took a real elephant ride. There was so much to see and enjoy for all ages.

During this visit, Ms. St. Denis took us on a tour of the parliament buildings in Ottawa. We visited certain rooms and went up to the big clock to see how it operated. Afterwards, we sat and watched the Royal Canadian Guards, dressed in their red uniforms, put on a dynamic show for the public. I was totally impressed with their marches. Later, we went to museums and looked at artifacts and prehistoric skeletons of dinosaurs. We went into rooms set up like theatres and enjoyed the sound and effects which were considered advanced technology then. Before our trip ended, Ms. St. Denis took us shopping. She bought us toys, colouring books, crayons, clothes, and shoes. As agreed, we bought a gift for mother and helped prepare her parcel. Ms. St. Denis was really good to both of us!

Towards the end of August, we were allowed to help her mother with minor chores. We would quietly sit on the floor and open pea pods, placing the peas in containers. Sometimes, we separated the green and yellow beans and placed them in their own baskets. Nothing was strenuous or stressful; it was a relaxing time. Mrs. St. Denis would sit in her chair, talking and working along with us. She always showed appreciation for the least little job we did for her. The autumn air filled their home with joy because the fruits of hard labour were manifested at harvest time.

The month went by fast. The night before leaving, I felt restless, got out of bed, and walked towards the open window. I took a deep breath of the fresh night air and gradually exhaled. I looked up at the diamond-studded sky and realized how happy I had been and how awful I felt about going back to St. Ann's. My mind had worked like a camera all summer, recording scenes that flashed before me: my sister and I dressed up in old clothes, washing the car, holding our dolls, showing off our little kittens, sitting under a shade tree at our little table, walking hand in hand with Ms. St. Denis. As I wiped my tears, I giggled to recall a day the three of us had walked to the mailbox. I felt a slight drop hit my face and looked up at Ms. St. Denis, asking, "Is it starting to rain?" She looked at me and started to laugh. "No, Mary," she said, and wiped my face really fast. It had been a bird dropping!

I went back to my bed and drifted to sleep, replaying the visit to Expo, the parliament buildings, the march of the Royal Guard, the museums, the shopping malls, and helping to prepare our parcel to Mother. It saddened me to know I would be leaving a family that accepted us and shared their love and genuine kindness.

A Second Term Served

When we got back to St. Ann's, Vivian and I learned I was being placed under Sister Greta with the big girls, and she would remain under Sister Deanna. It was a difficult adjustment because it was the first time we had been separated since we entered the school. I went through a second phase void of emotions and missed my sister terribly, although I had to learn to conceal it because I had seen what happened to the girls who expressed loneliness. It was totally unacceptable and a guarantee something would be done.

Sister Greta was fairly tall and very strong. This group followed rules like the other group. We were given our numbers and uniforms. What was a little different was that Sister Greta was not as strict with silence in the hallways or while doing chores. She did, however, ask us to keep it under control and at minimal volume. The only place she forbade talking was in the cafeteria and in our dormitory once we were in bed.

Unfortunately, the same "harsh corporal punishments" applied. Sister Greta was really rough. She would use her hand, open or closed, to hit or strike. She would hit with such force it caused nosebleeds and lacerations. This usually escalated into hair-pulling, grabbing and slamming heads on hard surfaces, dragging girls across the floor or down a few steps. Sister Greta would push girls around the room, shove them against walls, and throw them to the floor. It always bothered me to see her out of control.

I remember how I use to admire Queen Rita for her beauty. She had a pretty, angelic face. Her reddish-brown hair looked good even when it was messy. She was tall and had a very nice figure. If a modeling agency discovered her, she would have received instant recognition. Sister Greta had it in for her from the beginning. She did not need an excuse to hit her. I saw Rita beaten so many times, her facial features turned from soft and elegant to mean and hardened.

One small source of relief was a girl named Annie, nicknamed *"she-sheep,"* which means "duck." She was well liked by most of the girls and boys and something of a rescue person, especially when it involved Rita. Sister Greta did not care to have Annie around too much, probably because Annie stood up to her and would not be intimidated or manipulated. Whenever Rita was getting a beating, Annie would run and get help. She always managed to get someone else involved. I admired her for the bravery she demonstrated.

Annie took me under her wing, and I adopted her as my big sister. She had an inner strength which she shared with us, always making us feel good about ourselves.

She was genuine, never once making anyone feel obliged. I often wondered how she was able to deal with her own insecurities. Nevertheless, she made life bearable for me that year; if anyone tried to bully me, Annie put a stop to it.

There were, however, many other ways in which Sister Greta tried to hurt the students. For example, if the older children were going through the normal phase of attraction to the opposite sex, they were not able to share their affection because the girls were heavily scrutinized. Consequently, girls and boys kept in contact by writing notes. If the boy happened to be in another class, one of the girls would deliver the note. The boys would do the same thing. At times, the girls got careless and would lose notes. If Sister Greta found one, there would be a confrontation with the girl to whom it was sent. Sister Greta would read the note out loud for all to hear in order to cause embarrassment. The girl who was confronted would pretend to be remorseful and show some tears. In reality, the tears were a deterrent. As soon as Sister Greta was out of sight, the girl would break out into giggling.

That year, no matter how hard I tried to avoid it, I constantly fell into the wrath of Sister Greta. Three of us, Ellen, Louise, and I, were the youngest in the group. One morning, we showed symptoms of a cold. Sister Greta instructed us to stay in bed. Of course, we obeyed. We did really well but eventually got bored. So we whispered and convinced each other to race to one end of the dormitory, touch the wall, and run back. We all ran, giggling all the way and having a lot of fun. Eventually, we lost interest in that activity. So I talked the girls into jumping over the beds in the center aisle. The girls agreed. As I stood giggling, I noticed Ellen and Louise had stopped smiling. They both had a look of terror on their faces as they faced the door. The top of the staircase before entering our dormitory was always dark. I turned and my eyes focused on the silhouette of a nun. I swallowed hard, realizing it was Sister Greta. She had been standing there watching us. She came down the stairs towards us and slapped each one in the head. She marched us to her office, distracting the other entire girls who, by this time, focused their attention on us. Sister Greta made us wait outside her office. Shortly after, she came out with a pair of scissors and sat us down. One by one, she chopped our hair into crew cuts with bald patches. Public humiliation was our punishment. Some girls started laughing, but the older girls stopped them and explained that what was done to us was not a laughing matter.

I remember feeling so singled out. I had no place to hide and wanted to disappear. I felt really embarrassed and ashamed of myself for misbehaving. I did not realize that what Ellen, Louise, and I did was normal for kids. Once again, I found myself in a position where it was easier to function through my eyes. My emotions were frozen.

Another incident took place in the cafeteria. I remember all the girls were being punished. The meal was not served and we were to sit in complete silence. I got restless and started to fidget with my bread knife, figuring I was still sitting in silence. Without any warning, Sister Greta came up behind me and grabbed the bread knife, nicking the corner of my eye. Any closer to the centre would have been detrimental; thank goodness nothing serious happened.

I looked forward to night. It was a time for me to have a good private crying session, a place of refuge and tranquillity that Sister Greta could not take away from me. I could gather my thoughts without her interference. The question that always haunted me was, who would believe me? I remember falling asleep and feeling hate and bitterness toward all nuns, priests, teachers, and staff of the school.

When I woke one morning, I felt anger take root. I saw one of the girls, Laura, being slapped and was suddenly fed up with what we had to endure behind closed doors. If I was not being beaten, I stood around watching another girl being beaten. All were subject to some sort of violation or violence. I came to realize, at a very young age, that violence in movies was pretend while what was happening to us was real. After the incident with Laura, we all went to class, only I was not aware how upset I was. I remember Miss Johnson had asked me to sit down. I refused. She came towards me and tried forcing me down to my desk. Somehow, I pushed her away and managed to run out of the classroom and right out of the school. Fortunately, a worker in the field spotted me running. He yelled and I stopped, only to find myself in the cemetery. I wanted to be with dead people because I knew they were not going to hurt me. It seemed I had blacked out because I cannot remember running there. I recall looking at the school and feeling rage. I was out of breath and talking to myself. I said, *"It's okay, Mary. Sister Greta will beat you up and it will hurt for awhile."*

When I returned to the recreation room, word was already out about what I had done. Sister Greta was passing broken cookies around. I held my apron out. She looked at me and said, "You don't deserve these!" I glared at her until she dropped the cookies. Then I went back to class and apologized to Miss Johnson. She made me stand in the hallway facing the wall. I recall thinking, *"Did she have the right to grab me and try to force me to my seat? Why is she not apologizing to me?"* When I was allowed back into the class, I had to write another apology and a letter promising to behave. Something happened to me that day. I became hard.

Although I had prepared myself for a beating, Sister Greta did not lay a hand on me. From that time on, I noticed she was being cautious. She refrained from hitting or beating the girls. I believe this was partially because of the "annual visitors" who came frequently and made unannounced and unexpected visits.

I remember thinking that if a nun ever hit me again, only one of us would be left standing. I had no more to lose than what I had already lost. I had experienced every abuse one could never expect to live through. My dreams were wrecked and I could not imagine having a future. I lost my relationship with my siblings. I was so busy protecting myself, I suppressed my feelings. A piece of me died when I was betrayed by my guardians, by the very ones who were supposed to give me security and teach me to believe in myself.

Eventually, the school year came to an end. I remember standing by the swings, thinking, *"I entered this school a normal little girl. Now I am leaving with invisible scars. No one will ever know about the secrets born in the middle of nowhere, at a placed named St. Ann's Residential School in Fort Albany, Ontario."* Even though I stayed for just two years, a lot of damage was done in that time.

On my last evening, my thoughts were interrupted when *She-sheep* came and put her arm around my neck. She continued to hold me as we walked together towards the school and said our goodbyes. For some reason, I looked around and asked, "Annie, where is the horse that used to roam around here?"

She looked surprised. "Don't you know?" she said, and then added, with a flash of her teeth and the biggest smile I'd seen, "We ate it!"

Mary and Vivian at their St. Ann's Confirmation.

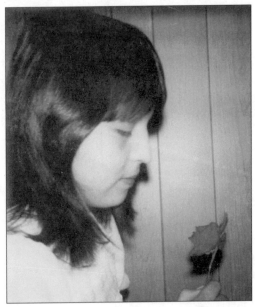

Mary and her rose.

Two very special people—Terry and Sean.

1989 Drug and Alcoholism Counselling graduate.

Killick's Corner

Meanwhile, back at our reserve, my mother had encountered more problems. She became the lady most talked about. Not only did the Chief and Council disagree with her going out and partying with other people from the reserve, they were also displeased that she was involved with a white man named Jim. His family emigrated from London, England when he was only five years old. Once in a while, mother would go to his place and do domestic or yard work, taking my brother, Michael, along.

The Chief and Council got upset and decided to evict her from her home on the reserve without the decency of notifying her. She was informed by one of her friends that her furniture, clothes, personal mementos, and pictures were gathered and trucked to the dump! Only two pairs of pants were left. She was also informed that her name had been omitted from the new housing list even though she was eligible. The Chief and Council were upset because she was leaving her home too frequently, but mainly because she was involved with a non-Native. Mother wanted to return to the reserve and ask them to reconsider, but Jim felt it was not a wise thing to do. Instead, he talked her into living with him, making an offer no mother could refuse—a home for her children.

Jim lived in a French settlement about thirty kilometers south of Hearst, in a town called Jogues. The area was known as "Killick's Corner," located on a concession off the main highway. His land was spacious and beautiful. It held a few buildings: a two-room bachelor house, outhouse, and a barn that stood alone in an open field with trees in the background which added to the scenic view. On top of the hill was a birch tree that became a favorite resting place for all of us. Down the hill was a creek that ran through the property; a big wooden bridge connected us to the main road. Further into the bushes was a spring that constantly supplied fresh water.

The living arrangement came as a surprise to us when we returned for summer holidays. At first, Jim and I disliked each other. It was the first time he had been involved with children, and I felt he might be trying to replace my father. One day, I watched him interact with my younger siblings. I noticed that, for a bachelor, he was really good to them. I was pleased and approved. We met each other halfway; he assured me he was not trying to take my father's place and understood he could never measure up to him or fit into his shoes. It was a realistic truce. Through the summer, he became an important figure in our lives. The house was small, but we gave it no thought and made the best of it because we were happy to be with our mother and each other.

My siblings and I had a very busy and active summer. We played in the barn a lot. Jim tied a rope, which was long enough for us to reach from the hayloft, to a beam and we would take turns swinging and dropping onto the bales of hay. On really hot days, we claimed a swimming spot in the creek. We used to spend the whole afternoon swimming, having water fights, and wrestling with each other. On other days, we played hide and seek, baseball, and cowboys and Indians. Sometimes, we would go for walks pretending to be on a treasure hunt in the old houses around the area.

Jim and Mother would take us for Sunday rides. Sometimes, Jim took my brothers fishing. Vivian, Mother, and I would stay home and give the house a good cleaning while everyone was out. Without really knowing it, Jim began to enjoy having us around. We dominated the fields with our presence and laughter. In the evenings, I would help Mother by washing my siblings. She prepared their snacks, and Jim would sit and listen as they shared the excitement of their day. Once my siblings were tucked into bed, they would quickly become calm and drift into sleep.

But our holidays came to an end and, once again, it was time to leave. That year, we were unexpectedly transferred to St. Joseph's Residential School in Thunder Bay. We departed from our home with an employee from the Indian Affairs office, who offered to provide us with transportation for the long trip. At least, that was the initial plan. Our driver was really proud of his brand new car. On the way to Hearst, my brother Johnny started playing with the window by rolling it up and down. Normally, I would have prevented him from doing that, but I did not say a word because I was upset to be leaving home and separated from my family again. I also dreaded going to a new school and having to readjust. My brother, who continued to play with the window, was distracting our driver. The driver turned to talk to him and lost control of his brand new car which began to swerve. He panicked and stepped on the brakes, causing the car to skid and slide into the ditch where it came to an abrupt stop. The front end was dented and steam was pouring out because the radiator was damaged. We all sustained minor injuries. My head banged on the dash, Vivian bit her tongue, and Johnny and Peter slid back and forth on the seat, causing them to collide into one another before they got slammed against the back. The driver hit his face on the steering wheel. The police came and we were taken to the emergency room, examined, and released. Even though we sustained minor injuries, our parents were not notified. The Indian agent got us a room for the night at the Waverly Hotel. The next day, he arranged our transportation by placing us on the bus.

Vivian and I always found something funny in those difficult times. In this case, a woman at the bus station had bought herself a new purse. She ended up giving Vivian her old one. Vivian took it just to show the lady her gesture was appreciated, but on the bus, we had a good laugh because she did not really want it. When we arrived in Thunder Bay, I told her to pretend to forget the purse on the bus. But when the driver began to inspect the bus after all his passengers disembarked, he discovered the purse and came running after us. We heard him yell, "Little girl!" but kept walking and pretending not hear him. He was persistent. "Little girl! Little girl! You forgot your purse!" Vivian and I had great difficulty keeping straight faces. She acted grateful and took the purse which, considering her size, could have passed for a suitcase. As soon as we got around the corner, Vivian asked, "Mary, what will I do with this? I don't want it!" I spotted a garbage can, and we started laughing uncontrollably. It took both of us to stuff the big purse into the garbage can!

A Place that Led Us Home

St. Joseph's Residential School served Native boys and girls from Long Lac, Armstrong, and Hearst. They also took in non-Native students from broken homes. It was not really a big school and not as strict as St. Ann's. We were allowed to leave the grounds and were transported to the school by bus as it was outside our residence. What St. Ann's and St. Joseph's had in common, was their harsh disciplinary measures.

One day, Donna, Susan, Laura, and me missed our bus to the school building. Right away, we were reported as runaways. We tried finding our way to the school but had no sense of direction and kept ending up on streets at which we had already been. It was getting dark, and we were getting scared. Several hours later, a couple of upset nuns came to look for us. They saw us wandering near the school. Without any warning, their car stopped in front of us to keep us from taking another step. We were surprised and relieved to see them but quickly shocked by our welcome. Sister Brenda jumped out of the car, grabbed Donna by the arm, and twisted it, then slammed her on the hood of the car. My heart began to pound as memories flashed before me. I remember thinking, *"Oh no, not again!"* Sister Johnson got out of the driver's side and stood nearby. Discreetly, she said, "Be careful, Sister Brenda, we're in public. Get them into the car. We'll deal with them at the school." When we were all in the car, I made an attempt to explain that we had missed our bus and got lost. They responded as if I was not there. Donna and Susan tried explaining, only to have Sister Brenda scream, "Shut up!"

When we arrived at the school, we were taken directly to the basement. We stood facing them. Sister Brenda grabbed Donna from the line. She barked, "You know what to do! Show them!" Donna stepped forward, raised her arms, and clutched the pipes that ran along the ceiling. Sister Johnson walked up behind her and pulled her pants down to her ankles. Donna was completely exposed from the waist down. Sister Brenda came along with a paddle stick that had a long enough handle to hold with both hands. She struck Donna repeatedly on the bottom. Donna cried and screamed each time she was hit. Her buttocks got red and welts formed before our eyes. Sister Brenda showed no mercy and continued to hit her.

The same harsh measures were taken against Laura and Susan. When it came to me, I faced them and said, "No one is going to pull my pants down!" Sister Brenda and Sister Johnson looked surprised, and then said, "Okay! No one is going to pull your pants down. But you have to hang onto the pipes like the others, and your hands will also be strapped." I obeyed. What the nuns did not know was that I wet my pants a little from the blows. When it was done, I turned around and stuck my hands out. As the stick whacked down on each hand, they became red and swollen. The nuns looked shocked that I did not scream or cry. When I realized I had wet my pants, I knew my spirit was breaking. Hardness took root. I knew I could not accept any more abuse.

Shortly after, I paid a visit to Mother Superior. I requested to be placed in a private home. At first, she did not take me seriously. I informed her that the nuns were too rough. I recall saying I could no longer ignore what was happening to the girls. She told me it was not meant to hurt us but to teach us to behave. I recall getting upset and telling her that I did not agree that anyone should be exposed in front of others while being spanked. Nor did I agree that I should be spanked until urine was forced out of me. I told her we had not been spanked for misbehaving but for honestly missing our bus and trying to find our way back. I also remember threatening to report the abuse to the police or the Children's Aid Society. Mother Superior listened attentively and asked me to give her time to make proper arrangements. Sister Brenda and Sister Johnson heard about my decision and knew I told of the incident that took place in the basement. They both were cold and deliberately shunned me, making me feel worthless. Shortly after, however, I was placed with a nice family for the remainder of the year. My mother got a bad report about me from the school which failed to mention that I got my way because I threatened them.

Living in a place with fewer restrictions felt like being released from serving time without ever committing a crime. I had great difficulty adapting to freedom and suffered a lot of uncertainty and stress. I remember coming out of the residential school convinced I was invisible and feeling inadequate. I always tried to be with students who were categorized in a lower class, because I could not help feeling that was where I belonged. I missed my siblings after leaving the school and tried to keep in touch with them. Sister Brenda and Sister Johnson, however, ordered me to have no contact with them whatsoever. It hurt a lot, but I had no choice but to comply. When the school year ended, I was relieved.

The following summer, I felt whole. Mother was shocked to see her younger children so thin. She always said that when the Indian agent told her, "I came to bring your kids home," they did not look like kids but like piles of bones. Later, I told her we had been in a car accident and placed, unsupervised, on the bus. My parents got angry that no one had made an effort to contact them, even if our injuries were minor. They had the right to be informed.

As usual, we had a splendid time as a family. Peter, Johnny, Vivian, and I always became withdrawn around August. The fear of returning to the residential school and being separated from one another bothered us. For some reason, my parents bought a bigger house that summer without any explanation. They had made the decision to keep us home and care for us. At first, I thought it was a dream. Jim, who I now called "Dad," told me while we were out on one of our treasure hunts that the employee from Indian Affairs had come to the house to make arrangements for our transportation back to the residential school. My parents joined forces and informed him of their decision to keep us home. The agent threatened to call the police, and Jim said, "Go ahead. I'm a taxpayer and you're off your territory. This is not a reserve. These are my kids now and they are here to stay. Not get out!" Dad said the agent was so stunned he left without saying a word. We were so happy and relieved to be together. Meanwhile, we had to remain in the bachelor house until Dad completed renovating the bigger house. We made no complaints as it was far better than being at the residential school. Before snowfall that year, we moved into our new house.

Being together as a family in a home became a reality when we began to live under one roof. We all needed to adjust to our new lifestyle. Although we were together, we kept our distance from each other because the separation in the residential school had affected the bonding of all our relationships. Dad, the bachelor, needed to adjust to becoming a family man. We were now his immediate family on a permanent basis. Mother needed to get used to having us around and to rebuild each relationship with her children on a personal level. Michael, the youngest family member, had to learn he was no longer the only child and get used to sharing everything. Peter, Johnny, Vivian, and I needed to adapt to being in a home rather than the institutional setting to which we had been accustomed. The overall goal was to respect one another's boundaries as individuals and to nourish the family unit. Even though it was difficult, the effort was worthwhile and we constantly worked at it.

We all took part in the operations of our home. Dad was the sole provider and supported all of us. Mother cared for the children and the house. My brothers got a fresh water supply daily. They helped my parents prepare wood for the winter, hauling and piling it in our woodshed. In the summer, they cut the grass. In the winter, they shoveled and kept the driveway clear. Vivian and I assisted Mother with weekly house cleaning and laundry. I did the ironing. My siblings and I took turns doing dishes after dinner. Mother and I bathed the children. My parents supported one another with cooking, shopping, and paying bills. It helped all of us to take on some of the responsibility.

That first year at Clayton Brown Public School, Michael enrolled in kindergarten. He was afraid and determined not to go. No one understood why he was behaving in such a manner because it was unlike him to react. Finally, I asked, "Michael, can you explain why you don't want to go to school?"

He answered, "Because I will not be able to come home after school." It had not dawned on us that he associated school with residential school.

I comforted and assured him by saying, "Michael, we will all be coming home after school." I recall how good I felt when the word "home" came out of my mouth. We took the bus to school and were all content knowing we would return at the end of the day. At first, the French kids did not make us feel welcome on the school bus. However, they gradually got used to us. Natives and non-Natives got along well at our school. All my siblings were pleased to meet up with their friends from the days before residential school. It took awhile to get settled in a regular routine and wasn't easy on any of us.

Blending into Freedom

I got along well with just about everyone I met. The problem was that I felt awkward and out of place. My peers liked me, but deep within I felt alienated and lacked a sense of belonging. This insecurity followed me after I left the residential school system and was a personal struggle I battled daily. I was able to keep it concealed. One day in class, I was asked, "Mary, what do you want to be when you graduate?" I could not honestly answer the question, because my dreams ended in residential school. I had been told repeatedly that I was too stupid to amount to anything and believed it. So I never expressed any of my dreams and aspirations; they were dormant.

When I returned to the public school system, I could not get used to the teacher talking to me as an individual. Teacher/student rapport was totally unfamiliar, because I was accustomed to teachers who talked down to me. I was used to dictatorship with no emotional attachment. Moreover, I had a poor attitude towards my academic achievement. I did my schoolwork aiming only to pass because I had been trained to believe my potential was unimportant and Indians should not expect to get good jobs, even if they had the education and credentials for the work force. My horizons were limited, because I carried my "residential school baggage." I had developed tunnel vision.

Towards the end of the year, a girl named Sally started picking on me. I was patient with her and managed to avoid the confrontations she tried to instigate. It was often a challenge to ignore her arrogance. One day, I went to class as usual and sat down. Sally deliberately bumped into my desk and knocked my books, pens, and pencils onto the floor. Her friends started laughing while I bent and gathered my belongings. I felt humiliated and looked at the sheepish grin on Sally's face. For a split second, I saw the face of Sister Deanna reflected in her. I panicked—my breathing became rapid and the dampness of sweat formed on my face. I grabbed her with one arm and flipped her over my desk. She lay on the floor, stunned, as I jumped on her stomach and slapped her face repeatedly. I grabbed her by the hair and slammed her head on the floor. She was crying and pleading for me to stop, but I couldn't. I was yelling, "Get up! Come on, get up!" I had her by the hair. Everyone was shocked. The boys finally came to their senses and pried me off her. I was very angry and showed no remorse as Sally cried. How could she expect to tease and humiliate me and get away with it?

We were both sent to the principal's office. I allowed her to speak first without interrupting her. I got insulted when she made herself sound like an innocent victim who was attacked by a wild woman. Mr. Donald looked at me with disdain, horror, and disbelief. He finally said, "I could suspend you for this! But since this is near the end of the school year, I won't."

"Typical," I thought. "He expects me to accept his generous decision?" I surprised myself when I interjected and refused to take sole responsibility for what had happened. I was more amazed when Mr. Donald listened attentively. In the end, Sally and I were justly corrected and dismissed. What scared me about the violence I had demonstrated was the enormous strength I had while in a rage and the way I showed no mercy or emotion at my actions. Sally and others never bothered me again.

After the fight at school, I began to change. I was afraid to sleep because my former supervisors—the nuns and priests—intruded my dreams. I would wake up in a sweat and trembling. One night, during a nightmare, I could not wake up. I screamed so loudly, I woke my dad who was hearing-impaired. He came running into my bedroom in his white long johns. Fred came racing in next in his gray long johns. I sat on my bed, gasping for air. My heart was pounding. I suddenly realized I was awake. Dad looked really concerned. He asked, "What was the nightmare about?" I avoided answering the question and said, "It's okay, it was a bad dream." I wanted to tell him about the abuses I had endured in the residential schools and that my abusers tormented me in my dreams every now and then. But I was too scared that no one would believe me and ashamed of myself. I could never tell anyone about it. My brother, Fred, said in his humourous way, "Look at it this way, Mary. You had two knights dressed in white and grey come to rescue you!" We all laughed. For the longest time afterward, I suffered from insomnia.

After this incident, I found ways to relieve my memories of torment. I would go for walks down the main highway and sit at the bridge. I would spend countless hours writing to my abusers. Then I would stand at the top of the bridge, lean over the rail, and watch my tears drop into the creek. I felt more release when I shredded those letters. I felt in control as I threw the pieces into the creek. I often used this method to release painful experiences that I wanted desperately to disappear. I had learned to keep my secrets with a tight iron fist! I could not allow my family to know what had happened to me.

Unfortunately, I had other problems to contend with. Alcoholism began to interfere in our home. It was not constant, but it gradually developed into a regular occurrence. My siblings and I did not like to see our parents intoxicated. It would upset and terrify all of us. Dad and Mother would fight, something they never did when they were sober. My siblings would cry and could not understand why our parents behaved that way. It had been a way for them to drown their sorrows while we were at school. But I felt there was no reason for them to drink now that we were home. To a degree, the residential school system enabled and justified many parents' alcohol consumption. Dad knew I refused to condone or accept alcoholism in our home, and it caused a showdown between us. I decided to go the whole nine yards, determined to have an alcohol-free home. It could be no other way. The memory of losing my natural father bothered me. I vowed I would not risk losing another parent that way.

I remember three incidents between my parents and I when they were intoxicated. What was odd, was that they never dealt harshly with me when sober. The first time my dad came home under the influence of alcohol, he was bothersome. He kept pestering Vivian. She was getting upset and did not want him near her, so I finally told him to leave her alone. He got angry with me and pushed me against the counter. I pushed him back. He came towards me again, shoving me. I tried getting away, but he managed to catch me and bend me over the counter, pressing my face down. I began fighting back and remember seeing a knife. Fred heard the commotion. He jumped between us and broke us up. I recall telling Fred and Mother that I wanted to stab him, and they were surprised by my cruel thought. The anger was turning to rage, and no one knew how serious I was.

The second incident was with my mother a few months after. My parents were both intoxicated. They had been drinking elsewhere all night and did not come home until the following day. Before they got home, I instructed my siblings to play outside until the coast was clear, mainly because I did not want them to get upset. My dad passed out on the armchair. Mother stayed up and asked me to cook breakfast for her. I cooked eggs, bacon, and toast and felt nervous as I served her the plate. As I turned to walk away, I heard a loud crack. Mother had thrown the plate of food on the floor. "Mom, why did you do that?" I asked and got on my knees to clean the mess. Mother came up behind me and held the back of my neck. I began crying and pleading for her to stop. I tried to get up, but she was too strong. She pushed my face into the food on the floor. A flash-back of the toilet incident at school had been revived. Mother stopped. I was crying, trembling, and feeling totally worthless.

Soon the drinking became periodical. It was beginning to affect us to the point where we dreaded our parents' trips to town. As time went on, I became more hateful and resentful. An unresolved past and the alcoholism in our home began to conflict with my efforts at school. I lost interest in everything and started skipping classes. Mr. Chad approached me about my marks. All I wanted was for my parents to quit drinking. I had beautiful parents, the kind which street kids could only dream of, and a home which street kids could never imagine. I wondered if my parents were going to take it all away from me and determined it would not happen without a fight. My parents, siblings, and our home were worth fighting for. Unfortunately, I could not disclose my problems at home because I was ashamed of the drinking. I began acting out to take attention away from my home.

One day after school, I wanted to get home because nothing had gone right for me that day. We all got on the bus as usual. Michael, my little brother, ended up towards the back of the bus because there was nowhere else to sit. He sat down with a girl named Lynn who did not want Michael next to her and pushed him off, causing him to fall on the floor. I saw red. No one was going to rough up or hit any of my young siblings. It was something I would not tolerate. I helped Michael off the floor and instructed him to sit on my seat. I sat next to Lynn and looked directly into her eyes, saying, "Try that on me." I was so angry my jaw tensed and my teeth were clenched. Lynn made a mistake when she slapped my face. In an instant, the vision of Sister Deanna flashed before me. I grabbed her by the throat and began to slap her repeatedly. Then I grabbed her hair and slammed her head on the window. Lynn's crying did not touch me. Everyone on the bus watched in horror.

Finally, another male student and the bus driver had to pry me off her. They literally had to use force to restrain me. When they grabbed me, the vision of Sister Deanna reappeared. I could not stop. I had lost control. What brought me back to my senses was they did not hit me. All they were trying to do was stop me from getting at her.

My siblings were impressed with what I had done. When I got home, I was upset and crying, not out of remorse, but because I had been restrained. My parents were angry with me at first. They also knew I would do anything to protect my siblings. When my siblings explained what had happened, my parents looked at each other and said, "No wonder."

Later that evening, Mr. Jacques, the owner of the bus line, paid me a visit. He informed me that Lynn's parents had made a complaint and indicated that a confrontation was going to happen sooner or later, even though he had told Lynn's parents to instruct her not to push anyone again. His defense of me came as a surprise. I assured him this was not going to happen again, emphasizing "provided no one hits or mistreats any of my siblings."

He answered, "I assure you, Mary, after what happened on that bus today, no one will bother you or your siblings again. You scared them. Even the three guys that restrained you were amazed at the strength you demonstrated."

I was astonished. That night as I lay in bed, my tears flowed freely. I knew I had to change because I was capable of seriously injuring someone when my rage escalated to the blackout state. When I returned to school the following day, I felt bad when I saw what I had done to Lynn's face. When I approached her to apologize, she jumped back and attempted to run from me. I said, "No, don't be afraid. I want to apologize for yesterday."

Lynn looked surprised and responded, "I'm sorry too. I had no right pushing your little brother that way." That day, I promised myself I would do my best to refrain from violence. I was determined to improve in other areas that needed work.

My parents and I continued to drift apart. I behaved at home so it would not be hard on my siblings. Although one could feel the tension between my parents and I, I continued to help with chores. I was a teenager and had changed. I began to hang around teens that drank. There was minimal progress with my marks at school. A couple of times, I ran away from home. It was a way for me to relieve stress. The last time I ran away, I vowed I would do better and change my ways.

One evening, my parents went to town and started drinking. They brought back a lot of people and decided to have a party at our home. I got fed up. I instructed my siblings to stay in the room while I joined the party. Everything was going well and everyone was enjoying him or herself. Betty, a lady at the party, became agitated with me for no reason. I was not even talking to her. I avoided her as much as possible, but she got everyone to conspire against me, including my parents. She came towards me. I tried to get away but was too slow because I, too, had been drinking. She grabbed me and hit me. The next thing I remember was Betty goading everyone to hit, punch, slap, or kick me. Everyone participated. She kept yelling, "give her a good beating." My siblings watched in horror, crying and screaming. I started yelling and begging them to stop, but they continued without mercy. My mind went blank; I could not face what was happening, neither could I believe or accept my parents' involvement. The next day, my siblings had such sadness in their eyes. I could not look at my parents and I knew I could no longer live there. Everything we had worked so hard for was broken and taken away from me.

I called my sister, Margaret, from school and asked if I could come and stay with her. She agreed to take me in. I did not bother to discuss my decision with my parents because I felt betrayed. All that week, I remember feeling lost and in such despair. My nights were torment. I awoke from nightmares of every abuse I had experienced in the residential school as well as the most recent beating in my home. I slipped into depression. At the end of the week, Vivian gave me a message that Mother wanted to speak with me. For some reason, we kept missing each other, so I went to her house.

The next day, Margaret asked if I was going out. I said I was and left the house until she and her husband, Randy, got on the bus to town. Then I went back to the house and searched for the nerve pills my sister had just had refilled. Without any thought, I downed fifty-four tablets. I wrote a suicide letter stating how tired I was of the drinking, babysitting, and nightmares of bad experiences in the residential schools. I was tired of being beaten. Seven hours later, my sister and her husband decided to come home. When they found me sprawled out on the coffee table, they thought I had been drinking.

Margaret was shocked to discover what I had done when she read my letter and realized I was in a coma. They called an ambulance and the police became involved because I was a minor. Doctor Jannings examined me and declared me in critical condition with minimal chance of recovery.

I remained on a critical list for one week. I would not respond to anyone except to a friend named Candice. When I was taken off the critical list, I saw a nun standing over me and remember thinking, "If only she knew!" I wanted the unpleasant memories to be erased. I was ashamed for not succeeding. I had lost my desire to live.

I was placed in a setting for troubled teens where I received counselling for my most recent problems although I did not disclose the residential school issues. The same question haunted me—"Who would believe me?" When I completed my treatment, I was placed under the care of Children's Aid for several months.

While I was away, Mother quit drinking. Dad continued until she confronted him and gave him an ultimatum. She said she was leaving because she no longer wanted her children around the alcohol. Dad cried and gave in, choosing the family he had become fond of. When I returned home, things were different. We began to heal as a family. Our respect for one another became very important and our boundaries grew solid. Without the drinking, our lives improved.

Fond Memories of My Siblings

As we all began to feel more content and secure, we developed a routine. After we did our chores, we would do various activities together. In the summer, we changed our swimming spot from below the creek to under the bridge. Sometimes, after regular swimming, water racing, and water wrestling, we would agree to bug the hornets. There was a hornet's nest along the bank, not far from our swimming area. We would throw rocks at it. When the hornets attacked us, we would dive under the water and wait for them to fly back to their nest. Outsmarting the hornets was a fun challenge because we always managed to escape their stings.

I remember when Edmond joined us at our swimming area for the first time. We had discovered a rock that we could dive off in the deep spot. Edmond asked if it deep enough and Peter, who was standing in the deep end, said, "Yeah! Dive in!" Vivian, Johnny, and Michael looked at each other with sheepish grins. Edmond neglected to consider his greater height and took Peter's word. He came back up with a scrape on his nose from the ridge to the tip. We all started laughing. It was comical at the time, but thank goodness nothing tragic happened.

The other play area was in the barn. Dad had tied a rope to the center of the beam so we could swing and drop onto the hay below. One day, Peter decided to show off. He swung fast without concentrating on the timing. We were all excited and cheered him on. He let go of the rope and flew right out the window, crashing onto the ground without any cushioning. We all laughed, forgetting, once again, to think of the possible consequences.

One afternoon, while we were in school, Michael disobeyed and my parents lost him. Dad went to search for him and found Michael snagged by the back of his collar on a nail. He had been hanging there helplessly until Dad took him down. My parents were upset, but we laughed. Another time, Michael got hurt when we were playing in the barn. He lacerated his head and required stitches. As usual, we laughed. My parents had the last laugh when they dismantled our barn.

Once in awhile, we played baseball together. My brothers would play football, but Vivian and I only joined them once because they were too rough. We would watch instead. When Vivian got bored, she got me going. I would chase her and when I caught her, I'd sit on her and pin her arms underneath my knees. When she could not move, I'd take a grass blade and stick it in her nostril to make her sneeze. Laughing, she would yell, "Mary! Don't!" I would call our dog, Timothy, to lick her face. Vivian was so immobilized, all she could do was move her head side to side to keep Timothy's tongue from her mouth. When she laughed and yelled, "Okay, Mary, that's enough!" I would say, "Are you telling me what to do?" Vivian would be laughing so hard, all she could do was yell, "Yes!" Then I would tickle her, to make her laugh harder. In the end, we would both be laughing.

Vivian and I also did acrobatics. I would lie on the ground and raise one leg. Vivian would grab my hand and place her foot on mine. Eventually, she would balance herself in a standing position on my upraised feet. Sometimes, I would either lie on the ground or stand and lock hands with Vivian. I would gradually raise my arms, holding her as she balanced herself in an erect position. We practiced a lot and had lots of fun.

Some of our activities included our parents. Mom and Dad would take us into the bush where Dad worked in our lot. He would cut the trees, peel the bark, pile the logs in rows, and sell them to contractors. Sometimes, he got us to help but made sure we had fun in what we were doing. My parents would pack a lunch and make a lovely picnic of it. Afterwards, we would play near the area they were working, laying bark on the ground to make a lane way. Then we would take turns slipping and sliding to the end. Dad and Mom would watch and laugh with us.

On sunny afternoons, Dad would take us for a nice long ride. We would enjoy the quiet time as we all admired the scenery. During berry season, we would go into the bush. Once, my dad said he knew an ideal spot for berries, so we all got into the car, including our dog, Tootsie. What Dad did not realize, was that the area had become a snake pit. We were not aware of it either until we disturbed them. Vivian stood by a skinny tree and wrapped her hand around it as she stopped to talk to

Peter. She felt something moving and released her hand, screaming, "Snake!" Then we heard Johnny and Michael screaming "snake" in a location not far from us. Mom and I ignored the screams and continued to pick blueberries. Then I felt something looking at me and saw a fair-sized snake stretched out on a tree nearby. I screamed "snake!" and Mother did not even bother to look; she just went running by me, screaming for dear life and leaving me behind. We all ran out of the bushes from different directions. Peter and Johnny had to race back to rescue Tootsie who had fallen into an old well and was barking like crazy. By the time we made it back to the road, Dad was bent over with laughter and had tears running down his cheeks. He said it was hilarious watching the expressions on our faces. What little berries we had had been dumped in flight and we went home empty handed.

Festive holidays became times we enjoyed as a family. At Christmas, Dad would take my siblings into the bush to get a tree which they would bring home on a sleigh. A few days before Christmas, our parents would take us into town to do some shopping. Sometimes Dad drove us, but one particular time we took a taxi. My siblings and I sang carols all the way home, and the driver enjoyed our singing, commenting, "A happy family."

On Christmas Eve, we would go to midnight Mass. My dad would stay home with Johnny and Michael because we felt they were too young and would get tired. Besides, it was usually too cold for them to be out. After Mass, Dad had our midnight snack ready. We would get Peter and Vivian settled, who would be fast asleep in no time. My parents and I would tidy up and place all the gifts under the tree. In the morning, we awoke to very excited children. They would not open of their gifts until everyone was up. Then, joy and laughter filled our home. My parents would prepare and cook our lunch. Once everything was ready, we sat together to eat turkey and all the trimmings.

Easter was another celebration my family enjoyed. My siblings' faces would glow as my parents gave each their bunnies, eggs, and candy. My parents always cooked turkey or ham. When everything was ready, we would sit together and enjoy the excellent meal our chefs prepared for us. By the end of the day, my parents and I were eager to get the hyper children to bed! But these occasions became precious memories for all of us.

My parents always made sure we had quality family time. Sometimes we watched television together. Other times they allowed us to play outside and later joined us for wiener and marshmallow roasts. On the weekends, our treats varied. Dad was an expert at popping corn on the stove. Sometimes they gave us pop and chips. During the winter months, they would get me to prepare a pizza or a cake. These were some of the activities that brought us close together.

There was also a serious side to our parents. My dad, the "non-Native," was a gifted man and could be defined as a "jack of all trades without any credentials." He was skilled at hunting, fishing, and trapping and always said "his boys" were going to be all trained in these areas. True to his word, my brothers, Edmond, Peter, Johnny, and Michael acquired these skills. They had a good mentor in Dad, who took the time to teach them proper methods and demonstrated his abilities. The other area our Dad took time to teach us, was gardening. Every year, we planted potatoes, radishes, green onions, and carrots. My parents also made a beautiful flower arrangement that was admired by all who drove by Killick's Corner!

Personal Growth

Although my home life improved immensely, my past at the residential school haunted me. There were times I came close to disclosing it, but the fear of trusting a person always prevented me. Externally, I gave the impression there was nothing bothering me. Internally, the anguish was brewing and festering. At the prime time of my life, I was really insecure about my personality and physical appearance.

I was well liked by people of different age groups and had no problem making friends, but often wondered what people saw in me and questioned why I was liked. Drinking alcohol became a way to escape my personal torments. I was never a promiscuous type. Some guys respected me for it while others despised me. I believed that an intimate relationship should be shared with someone special in marriage. I did not want to be used for a one-night stand because a lot of my friends were used that way. While the girl cried, the guy would laugh and brag to all his friends. I knew it was something I could not handle, so I prevented it from happening to me.

That year, I met Jason whom I liked a lot. All we ever did was drink and hang around with a group of friends. It was more of a companionship. He was a nice guy, but I never let him get too close to me. One night, he went to spend time with the guys and I met up with the girls. Late in the evening, my friend, Janet, handed me a key to a motel room. "If you want to see Jason, he will be waiting for you there," she said.

I said "okay," but felt uncomfortable with the change of plans. Jason usually consulted me. I got worried about him, so I left my friends in the bar to go and check up on him. As I entered, the bathroom light was on. I heard snoring and thought Jason had passed out. It was unusual for him to be in bed so early on a weekend. I flicked on the table light and was shocked to discover Jason completely naked with Doreen. I felt cheated and betrayed and left the room, knowing I would never bother Jason again.

The next day, Jason approached me and asked why I was avoiding him. I looked at him and wondered how he could question me. I was not going to tell him what I had seen. "It's over between us. There is no more 'us.'" He looked shocked and surprised, but I did not give him a chance to respond. I walked away feeling unwanted and very unattractive. After our break up, I saw Jason at the parties I attended. Sometimes he had a date and would embrace and kiss in my presence, or, out of spite, kiss any girl that was there. I showed no emotion. As far as I was concerned, he had crushed my feelings and violated our friendship. I filed him along with other abusers in the back of my mind and remained alone for awhile.

I began to enjoy going into bars and to parties by myself. One evening, I went and sat with Jane and Bert, a couple Jason and I used to hang around with. Jane wanted to discuss our break up. I looked at her and said, "I do not want to discuss it nor am I interested in reuniting with Jason." She apologized and dropped the topic. Bert felt bad and did not say much.

Suddenly, a tall and fairly attractive stranger came to sit with us. He knew Jane and Bert, so they introduced him to me as Clyde. He informed me he was new in town and came from Halifax, Nova Scotia. I enjoyed the small talk and thought nothing more of it. For a split second, I wished I was sitting at the birch tree on the hill, admiring the scenic beauty and listen to the sounds of water rushing down the creek. I thought out loud, saying, "Isn't nature beautiful?"

Clyde responded, "Yes! It is!" The next thing I knew, we were talking and laughing and really enjoying each other's company. During the evening, we discovered we lived eight miles from each other. From that evening, the casual acquaintance became a part of my life.

Clyde and I started dating regularly. We did lots of walking and spending relaxing evenings by open fires. Our relationship blossomed as we spent more time together and less time with friends in bars. My relationship with Clyde was different than any other I'd experienced. He accomplished what no one ever had by entering my heart, my sacred domain. Several questions kept racing through my mind: What did he see in me? What possessed him to be attracted to me? How did he manage to motivate me to consider my emotions when they had been so unimportant to me? What type of influence did he have over me? Why did he make me feel so very secure? Once Clyde became important to me, I let go of all the negative feelings I had towards myself. It was something I struggled with constantly. Several months later, as Clyde and I sat out in the moonlight, we decided to get married.

We talked to my parents about our decision. They were reluctant at first but gave in when they saw how determined we were. Clyde's mother, Bernice, made a special trip to Hearst to convince Clyde to reconsider the marriage proposition. When I first met her, I was not impressed. When we were with Clyde and his sister, Dorothy, she talked as if I did not exist. Bernice put me down and expressed continual rejection toward me. I wanted to walk out on her, but Clyde told her about the medical problems I was experiencing. The only reason he told was because Bernice was a Registered Nurse. She was blunt and diagnosed me with "Kissing Disease." With her very insensitive answer, she reopened my scars and made me feel cheap. I just sat there and took her insulting comments. I promised myself I would never give anyone the satisfaction of seeing me angry or trying to force me to walk out.

After our unpleasant meeting, Bernice instructed Clyde to come alone the following day. Clyde sensed I was upset and held me as we sat in the back seat of the taxi when he took me home that night. I was happy when the taxi pulled into my driveway and I rushed to get out. I looked up at the sky. The moon was shining, and the stars were twinkling. I walked towards the birch tree and sat down. The water rushing down below touched my spirit. I broke down and cried uncontrollably. I could not understand how Bernice could judge me without getting to know me. As difficult as it was, I admitted honestly that I did love Clyde and wanted to spend the rest of my life with him. Several months later, we got married without his mother's blessing.

During this time, my medical condition worsened. Clyde and I knew something was seriously wrong. My body was not responding as it should, and I frequently became weak and tired. A fever would rise without warning, my body would ache, my face would break out in open sores around the chin area, the corners of my mouth would have slight cracks, and my weight declined rapidly. I became more alarmed when I noticed it was a strain to climb stairs, steps, and curbs and to get up from sitting on a chair, couch, bed, and taking a bath. I struggled to get to a standing position. Some days were more difficult. While walking, I would suddenly lose my balance and fall. My arms did not have the strength to react and break the impact.

These symptoms were deceiving because they could appear or disappear at any time. At the onset, I went to see my doctor who treated me for the flu and vitamin deficiency. When the medication did not seem to improve my condition, I returned to the doctor to re-evaluate the situation. Finally, when the doctor could not pinpoint a credible diagnosis, I was told I had developed a psychological problem. That discouraged me and I stopped seeking medical attention although my condition worsened. I was frustrated with the whole ordeal, but Clyde was so very supportive. I used to cry and say, "Clyde, all I want is my health back." He would embrace me and say, "It's okay, hon. You will get well again."

Instincts of Motherhood

One day, Clyde came home all excited because a new doctor had opened an office in town. I reluctantly agreed to go. Doctor Windles' office was located on the second floor of one of the oldest buildings on the busiest street. I looked up at the steep staircase and wondered if I would be able to get up it. When I reached the landing, I was exhausted. Doctor Windles' secretary offered me a chair which I refused because I knew I would have to struggle to get to a standing position.

As the doctor examined me, he was astonished to see how weak I was. "How long has it taken you to get this weak?" he asked.

"It's been a very slow process, about two years."

"Why did you not see a doctor?"

"I did, and was treated for flu virus, vitamin deficiency, and later told it was a psychological problem. The doctors never took me seriously."

He looked disgusted and said, "Well, I'm admitting

you to the hospital. We need to do some tests." I gave a sigh of relief. Finally, something was going to be done. I went straight to the hospital. When Clyde came to visit me that evening, he looked more at ease.

After three days in the hospital, Doctor Windles came to express concern. He said, "Mary, when was the last time you had your period?"

"About three months ago. Why?"

He ignored the question and asked, "Is your period usually regular or irregular?"

"Irregularity is normal for me."

"Very abnormal and very unusual," he responded.

"Why would you say that?"

"Well, you're pregnant!" he said. "What concerns me is this pregnancy can cause a lot of complications." I looked at him, surprised. He took my hand and said, "Mary, there is a serious medical problem. Don't get your hopes too high with this baby." Tears rolled down my cheeks. He said, "I'm making further arrangements for you to see a specialist in Toronto who will tell you more about this. I've said more than I should have."

All I could think was, "Clyde and I are going to have a baby!" I was overjoyed. When Clyde came for a visit that evening, I gave him a brief update on the doctor's report. He went through the same shock I had experienced and said, "baby?" He was happy and concerned at the same time.

That night, my world came crashing down on me. My unwanted visitors entered my dreams, something I had not experienced since the start of my new life. I woke up in a cold sweat with my entire body trembling. "Clyde," I cried to myself, "how can I ever tell you? I have to keep it buried. You've already made me forget. You can erase the rest of my bad memories."

I was referred to Doctor Hunts, a neurologist at North York General in Toronto, and remained there for almost a month. During that time, I went through extensive testing and felt scared, lonely, and insecure. To make matters worse, Doctor Hunts gave a bleak report on my pregnancy. He came in one afternoon to convince me to have an abortion. I was stunned and flatly refused. I wondered if this was God's way of punishing me for my behaviour. "What's was the worst thing that can happen to my unborn child?" I asked.

"The medication you require can give the baby severe deformities," Doctor Hunts replied.

"Like what?"

He watched my expression as he carefully gave me an example. "Well, if it's a boy it can end up with female organs, or if it's a girl it can end up with male organs." I looked at him with disbelief and horror. He responded very quickly, "That's a worst-case scenario. But there could be other types of deformity."

"I don't know if I could handle an abortion. It's so final! What are my chances of having another child?" I asked.

He looked at me and said, "Nil. Because of the seriousness of your condition, I would strongly recommend a hysterectomy."

Numbly, I asked, "You mean, no other baby whatsoever? Isn't there something else we can do?"

"We can get an obstetrician to review your case," he replied.

With a sigh of relief, I agreed. "Yes, that would be fine."

Before Doctor Hunts left, he said, "Mary, prepare yourself in case he recommends and abortion, okay?" He must have known I had no intention of considering it.

When the doctor left, my heart ached as a mother. Some women think you become a mother after the baby is born. I learned very early that is not true. Clyde and I were already parents during my pregnancy. My motherly instincts were activated while the baby was developing in my womb. I thought things through very carefully because any decisions were crucial to my unborn child. That day, I roamed around the halls and wondered what the other specialist would be able to do for us. Without Clyde at my side, I felt alone and was restless and worried when I lay on my bed that night. For the first time in years, I got on my knees and prayed. "God, I know you're there. I need your help. The doctor thinks I should abort the child in my womb but he or she is already precious to me. I want you to help me carry my baby to full term, perfectly developed." Tears were running down my face. Reluctantly, I added, "I will try to stop hating those who caused me so much pain in the past." The tranquility I felt was refreshing assurance that God was listening. I wiped my tears and got back into bed. I rubbed my abdomen and said, "Baby, let's give this a good fight together. You're going to be a miracle baby, perfect in every way." I felt a little movement inside and knew I would carry my baby to full term.

The next morning, Doctor Hunts came with Doctor Patrick and Doctor Woo—specialists in gynecology and obstetrics—and they stood by my bed. Our conversation was brief and to the point. I eagerly asked what they thought. Doctor Patrick said, "It is possible for you to have your baby! What we will do is allow the fetus to completely develop. Then Doctor Hunts can prescribe the medication you require."

"Will my baby be deformed?" I asked.

"The worst that can happen is a hair lip. That can be rectified with surgery. The other problem is you will not be able to breast feed your baby because your milk will be contaminated by the medication." It was a small price to pay and I was relieved to hear such a positive report. As he was talking to me, I thought, "We will not accept even the hair lip." I felt encouraged that my baby was out of the danger zone.

Doctor Patrick said, "Doctor Woo and I will be monitoring your pregnancy. We highly recommend you give birth here."

I was elated and said, "Okay!"

When the specialists left, Doctor Hunts remained and said, "Mary, I'm glad this part has worked out for you. There is something else I wish to speak with you about."

The Diagnosis

He took a chair and sat beside my bed. "I got most of your tests back."

"Oh yeah! What is wrong with me?" I asked.

"I would rather tell you when all the tests are returned in a couple of days. Will your husband be down this weekend?"

"Yes, he said he would."

"Good, because I don't want you to be on your own."

I did not care for his serious tone. "Is it that bad?"

"Like I said, we have to wait for the other tests." Sensing my frustration, he added, "I know Mary. You have been through a lot already. Just be patient, okay? This condition is usually caused by high stress levels trigged by traumatic experience. Is there something you have experienced that is troubling you?"

I was surprised and avoided eye contact. Scenes of the past flashed before me. "No," I answered nervously.

Doctor Hunts noticed I was reluctant to speak. "If you need to talk to someone, we have very good counsellors and psychologists here." I could not believe what I was hearing. He noticed I was preoccupied and broke the silence by saying, "I just want you to know that help is available if you need it."

I said, "okay," but knew I was not ready to open my past to anyone. The shame and fear imprisoned me. By the time Doctor Hunts left, my hands were shaking and tears were forming in my eyes. I choked them back and refused to give in.

Clyde came that weekend. He was really pleased that our baby would be fine, but we were both eager to hear the results of my diagnosis. Not knowing was torment. Finally, Doctor Hunts arrived. "Mary," he said, "I have received all your test results. You have been diagnosed with polymiocitis which is a deterioration of muscle and a breakdown of your immune system. It could be life-threatening if it attacks the heart and lungs. The good news is, it is treatable. The bad news is, it is incurable."

I looked at Clyde. He was taking the news harder than I was. "What is it caused by?" I asked.

"It's very rare, and no one knows how it starts. It is a severe form of arthritis." Doctor Hunts broke the medical term into three parts: "*Poly* means 'many,' *mio* means 'muscles,' *citis* means 'inflammation.' And, unfortunately, there is more bad news."

"How can things get worse than they already are?" I thought.

"You will have to take high doses of cortisone which is the only medication available for this condition. It has some bad side effects. You can end up with "moon face," a roundness that distorts your natural features." I looked at him and rolled my eyes in disgust. He continued, "Or you could end up with a hunched back."

My mouth clenched. I was unsure what to say. I looked at Clyde who seemed to have gone numb and was showing no reaction. Finally, I asked, "How long will I be like this?"

"For the rest of your life, Mary. It is incurable."

"When can I go home?" I interrupted.

"Maybe in a couple of weeks, but I want you to be monitored while the treatment begins." I wanted to cry. Doctor Hunts gave Clyde and I day passes so we could go out. We were preoccupied with the diagnosis and yet avoided talking about it. We both disregarded the seriousness of my condition and focused on "our baby."

Although the ordeal was strenuous, Clyde was very supportive. I had a difficult pregnancy. I was sick and irritable and felt cheated because, now that I had found happiness with the man I loved, I was constantly tormented by the thought of losing it all. We lost the certainty of a future together. I resented my past and refused to tell Clyde about it when it should have been something I could trust him with. My instincts warned me against it. Perhaps I suspected he would not be able to handle it. My focal point became the baby who was worth fighting for and gave me a reason to live. If anything happened, it was the greatest gift I could give my husband.

After numerous monthly visits to Doctor Hunts, he thought I was close to giving birth. By early November, 1975, I began to have labour pains. Even though Doctor Patrick had recommend I deliver my baby in Toronto, labour persisted and Clyde had to take me to the hospital in Hearst. There they referred me to the larger hospital in Thunder Bay in case of complications.

My sister, Margaret, and her friend, Doreen, volunteered to drive us to Thunder Bay. We hit the first snowstorm of the year en route. When we arrived in Nipigon, my water broke. My sister comforted me and got me to relax. Every one of us was nervous and the storm intensified the tension. Surprisingly, we made it to Thunder Bay where they were expecting us. I was rushed to the maternity ward. Clyde looked worried; his facial muscles were so tense, it looked as if his jaws were clamped shut. I wanted to laugh. I wanted to cry. I did not know what to do. Clyde held my hand which meant a lot to me. We had gone through so much in such a short time. The doctor in Thunder Bay contacted Doctor Hunts who insisted I be transferred to Toronto. The labour pains subsided. The next day, Clyde and I were taken by air ambulance to North York General.

After a few days, my labour pains began again. The problem was, I could not dilate. Doctor Patrick and Doctor Hunts figured it was best to wait for natural birth to take its course. They prescribed something for pain but it only lasted temporarily. I heard other women screaming but refused to put Clyde through that experience, so I cried silently.

One nurse had gone off duty for two nights. When she came back, she was surprised to find me still in labour. I was crying. She looked alarmed and asked, "Have they given you anything for the pain?" I shook my head, gasping from pain. My eyes were red and swollen from crying. She looked at me with compassion and said, "Well, I don't care if I get fired. I'll get you something.

This is crazy!" Suddenly, she stopped and looked at me. "Oh no! You need immediate attention!" I heard her give a code over the intercom.

Nurses came running. They grabbed my stretcher and rushed me into the delivery room. Everyone was efficient. The nurse that helped me kept saying, "She's not dilating. Even if she's induced, she's too weak." Finally, Doctor Patrick said, "Okay, Mary, we have to do a C-section." I was given an anesthetic and the pain ceased. The doctors were talking about my baby. Suddenly, one said, "There he is!" I could not believe it was actually happening. Doctor Patrick said excitedly, "Mary! It's a perfect boy—five fingers on each hand, five toes on each foot. Not even a hair lip!" I was so relieved. At seven pounds and half an ounce, Sean was my pride and joy. Clyde was delighted to have a son who could carry on the family name.

Several months later, Sean's grandmother sent him a cup with his name's interpretation on it: "a gift from God!"

New Career

Clyde was employed with the Algoma Central Railway and had become dissatisfied with it. He was a graduate and wanted more security to provide for his new family. When everything settled down, he decided to join the Canadian Armed Forces. The idea bothered me, but once Clyde made up his mind to do something, there was no changing him. He went for his test, passed, was recruited and sent to Camp Borden, near Barrier, Ontario, for basic training. When Clyde left, I stayed with my parents until he sent for us.

I felt insecure and wondered how I would manage without him. Here I was, a young mother at the age of twenty, alone to care for a seven-month-old baby. I wanted to be with Clyde and, even though I knew his absence would be temporary, it felt like eternity. I spent a lot of time caring for our son. Once, as I was changing him, I thought out loud, "Okay, my baby-man, it's me and you from now on." From that time on, I became stronger and more independent. Clyde sent for us three months later. I was uncertain about the career change and the type of setting in which we would be living. Something gnawed at and annoyed me about it.

I got on the bus with my son. He was easy to look after and easy to please. Just as long as his tummy was filled, his diaper was changed, and he had his little toys with him, he was content. When we arrived in Barrier, Clyde was nowhere in sight. I panicked, thinking, "What if he doesn't show up?" Here I was, girl from a hick town with an infant in tow and very little money, in the middle of a fair-sized city full of strangers. I was so relieved when Clyde walked in. He was pleased to see us but also looked worried. He had not found an apartment for us. "What are we going to do?" I asked.

"Don't worry, I'll arrange something."

We stayed at a motel not far from the base. Before the weekend was over, Clyde found a place for Sean and I only. He had to remain at the base during the week. I was disappointed and had problems adjusting to life on my own, which probably had more to do with culture shock than anything else. I wanted to go home. I also noticed that when Clyde and I were together, there was tension between us. Once in a while, I would get angry and burst into tears. It seemed liked everything in my life moved at a rapid pace. I was amazed with the changes that had unfolded. Sean, at least, was very inspirational.

My joy when Clyde completed his training was only to be disappointed when I learned he had more training to do in Greenwood, Nova Scotia. "First the big city," I thought, "and now right of the province? Am I capable of doing this?" Clyde made it infinitely worse when he informed me I would be living with his mother. I reluctantly agreed to go. Eleven-month-old Sean paved the way for me because Bernice was happy to see her first and only grandchild. I still felt rejection from her. She made me feel uncomfortable. In the end, we compromised and made the best of living together. After all, it was only for three weeks and I would get to see Clyde on the weekends.

I missed Clyde and my family back home. Although, my sisters-in-law were good to me and kept me busy, I felt no sense of belonging, like I was intruding on a territory in which I was not wanted. One afternoon, the girls took Sean out for a long walk. I was alone with Bernice. She had a strong Gaelic accent and said, "I'm glad we can have this time together. I wanted to apologize for my ignorance and rudeness towards you." I was surprised and tears formed in my eyes. She smiled. "When my son told me he was marrying an Indian girl, I thought he was marrying a commoner. I have been watching you and you impress me. You seem to be a well-trained young lady and definitely a good mother. I was scared of you because I thought your people practiced witchcraft."

A sense of compassion came over me. I looked at her and said, "Don't worry. I would not know anything about it. I was trained by strict nuns in a residential school."

She sighed and said, "I feel so silly." We both laughed. Suddenly, she became very serious and said, "There's something I've been meaning to tell you about your new family. My son was exposed to years of violence while growing up. It did not stop until he was fifteen. His father beat me, but I stayed for the children."

"Clyde said something about it," I replied. "He never told me how long it happened, though."

She replied, "I know my children don't like talking about it. What I want you to know is that my son may have inherited a violent streak." We sat quietly for a few seconds. Then, "Mary," she continued, "don't take the abuse if it happens. Get out! Abuse can damage you, especially with your health condition. It worries me."

"Why are you telling me this?" I asked.

"The secret of the abuse that went on in our home needs to be told. I want to see the violence stop in this new generation. I'm not telling you this to scare you. I love my children. I think I did more harm by keeping them in it."

"Was alcohol involved?" I asked.

"No! My husband just abused me. Eventually, I ran out of excuses for my bruises, so I started telling others about it."

I admired her honesty. "Okay. I'll keep that in mind."

She looked relieved, knowing I believed her. "Look around this house. I bought everything myself, except the television, the car, and the building. My husband was too cheap to spend money on me, so I went back to work and purchased each item, piece by piece. I thought it was pointless to have a house without any furniture!" We both laughed.

The couple of hours we spent together were nice but odd. I thanked Bernice for the courage she demonstrated and for sharing such sensitive information. Our relationship improved, and I admitted she was a caring person underneath her hard front.

That weekend, Bernice and I went to Clyde's graduation while Sean stayed with close family friends. I was pleased to see how charming Clyde looked in his uniform. The graduates put on a dynamic show. When the ceremony was over, I reached for Clyde's hand while we were walking together. He pulled away and snapped, "Don't do that while I'm wearing my uniform!" A surge of hurt rose in my heart, especially when his mother said, "That's right, not while in uniform." I didn't say a word but thought to myself, "Who is in the service here? What's wrong with showing affection for my husband? Does he have to be naked?"

After graduation, we stayed with his family in Halifax for a couple of days. Then we went back to Hearst and picked up the rest of our belongings. Clyde had been posted in Cold Lake, Alberta. I thought it wouldn't be that bad because Clyde would be with me. I was wrong. He was not only at work all day, he also took on a part-time job in the evenings. I had a difficult time admitting we were drifting further apart. I was alone with Sean the majority of the time. The rigid life style bothered me: numbers were assigned for identification, men and women marched around like zombies, expressionless and emotionless. The coldness and the unfeeling environment made me cringe. I tried making friends but heard continual racist remarks and jokes about Natives who lived in a reserve nearby. Clyde was almost always gone. Occasionally, I would cry to him and tell him I was having a difficult time adjusting to our new lifestyle. Instead of comforting me, he pushed me away.

I did a lot of crying that year. Clyde had a life and he continued to live it. I did not get the support I needed from him. We had a few good times, but they were rare. Being alone constantly made me realize the career change had not been for us, but for Clyde himself. No doubt we were important to him at one time, but he changed when he went on his own. He was no longer a family man. He began to enjoy being by himself. It was difficult to accept that I was getting defeated and exhausted from losing the thing closest to my heart—my marriage.

I began slipping into depression and withdrawing into myself. Dreams of the past recurred. My sleep was tormented by nightmares. The next thing I knew, Clyde and I began to get into heated arguments which exploded into violence even with no alcohol involved. Each time Clyde hit me, images of nuns and priests in my past would flash before me. I would panic, forget where I was, and strike back, just as hard. Violence always triggered residential school experiences to the point that I associated him with the abusers of my past.

By this time, our marriage was hanging by a thread. We agreed to go for counselling. The problem was, the "priest" we went to ended up being biased and chauvinist. I was blamed for all our marital troubles and Clyde came out smelling like a rose. It sent more bitterness and resentfulness to my heart. Once again, a priest violated my life. His advice just caused more strain.

Finally, I came to terms with what was bothering me. It was a shock to realize that our present military lifestyle reminded me of life in the residential school. There were few differences between them. I needed to heal and that would certainly not happen at a base. Still, I did not share my past with Clyde. I asked him if I could go home for a visit. I needed to take a serious look at our marriage because it was no longer just the two of us. We had to consider an innocent third party—our son, Sean!

Escaping with Consequences

On my way back home, I began to relax. I had become accustomed to bearing sole responsibility for Sean. We were close. I understood his baby talk and had become a pro with his body language. He was an easy baby and enjoyable to travel with.

Once we were out Alberta, we transferred to another plane. As we were standing in line to get to our seats, the line slowed and came to a stop. I tried to see what was going on, but there was a taller man in front of me. Someone said, "A lady dumped her purse." I was about to take a step forward when I heard a woman cry out, "Oh my gad! She scalped him." People started laughing and I turned to look at Sean. He had something in his hand. To my surprise, it was a toupee! I wanted to laugh but had to refrain for the sake of the little bald man who stood up with a bright red face. He looked as embarrassed as I was. By this time, Sean had decided he was not going to give up the new toy without a fight. His little hands gripped it very tightly. Eventually, the little man got his toupee, mangled with baby saliva.

I was laughing uncontrollably when I got to my seat. Tears rolled down my face. What had made the incident more comical was the gentleman's wife, who stood up and slapped his bald head. "I told you to put it on securely," she said. "What do I have to do, staple it to you?"

When we arrived in Trenton, a young serviceman looked over at me and said, "Allow me to help you carry him. Lord knows what he'll grab next!" I followed, laughing.

My family was anxiously waiting to greet us in Hearst. I was glad to see them and realized how much I had missed them. Home released me from the constant reminder of my past. Moreover, I did not miss Clyde as much as I previously had. Too much had happened between us and remained unresolved. My parents knew I was exhausted, mentally, emotionally, and physically. They helped with Sean and I got to catch up on sleep.

As the visit came to an end, however, the old feelings I experienced before leaving for residential school surfaced. I became nervous, anxious, and restless. I took a walk to the bridge Clyde and I made our special place and pleasant memories came back. I began crying because I knew I desperately needed help. I was confused and questioned if my marriage was worth fighting for, asking myself, "Am I the only one whose is supposed to work at it?" I knew I could not do it alone and admitted I was in a very delicate state. I decided to extend my stay. Clyde had not called me since I left home, fuelling the decision. I needed to get myself well before I could work on our marriage. I needed counselling. I used a pay phone in town to speak with Clyde privately. When I asked if I could stay a little longer, he got angry. "You're my wife," he yelled, "and you're going to do as I say. Now get your butt on the bus and get home."

"Clyde, I can't. I need to go for...."

"What do you mean you can't?" He tried remaining calm but the tone of his voice was obvious. I held the phone away and started crying, sobbing, and shaking. "Please Clyde, try to...." He interrupted me again. Finally, I raised my voice and said, "Listen to me for a minute. I'm concerned about our marriage."

He responded sarcastically. "Now you've got the idea. Get on that bus and get home!" I continued crying. If I had been home, this would have ended in violence. For an instant, I felt defeated. I remember thinking, "I can't live like this. All my life I have been subject to abuse. I can't go through any more." Clyde was scream-ing and swearing, so I hung up. I waited for about fifteen minutes before calling back. He was calmer. "Okay. You can stay. When will you be returning?" he said.

"Maybe in a month. I need...."

"Are you crazy?" he shouted.

"I don't know. I think I'm getting there. I have to...."

Clyde refused to listen and ignored everything I tried to tell him. He became stern and said, "Quit this non-sense. Get your butt home."

I remember feeling emotionally torn. Then anger rose. "No!" I yelled back. "You're forcing me again. This time, it's not going to work!" I hung up, knowing I could not convince him. Besides, he didn't even consider how rudely and aggressively he was treating me. Swearing had becoming his natural way of speaking to me, the very person he was supposed to care about and cherish. I walked away crying, wishing that we could make a decision together. It was his way or no way! Not once did he consider how I supported him during his career change. It seemed I was always alone. He was a good at providing my basic needs but terrible at considering my mental and emotional well-being.

I was in a mess—confused and very insecure. Although the problem had been identified, in reality, I was festering away. It was beginning to interfere with every area of my life. I made up my mind to deal with the problems, with or without Clyde's support. I knew I was taking a risk and had a lot to lose, but I wanted my private hell extinguished once and for all.

After a month at home, Clyde made no effort to phone and check up on us. I had gone to four counselling sessions and was beginning to feel good about myself. I called Clyde, who was not really pleased to hear from me, wanting to tell him about the counselling and that I was showing progress. "When are you coming home?" he asked.

"Soon!"

Suddenly, he shouted, "What is going on up there? Have you got a boyfriend?"

I was stunned and surprised by how poorly he thought of me. "Yeah! I got a boyfriend," was my sarcastic reply. I was sorry I said it because he didn't give me an opportunity to rectify it. "Are you leaving me?" he snarled.

"No!" I insisted, getting nervous. "I'm going for...."

"I'm coming to get Sean," he interrupted, knowing he had touched a nerve.

I felt frightened and screamed, "You can try! I'm the only parent he has known since he was seven months old! You'll never, never have him." We were both screaming and cursing. I felt so disgusted, I hung up. Clyde did not like to lose. I knew he was going to use force to get to me. I could not see why he wanted me home because he was never there.

I walked away feeling very angry. Suddenly, I saw my sister, Margaret, who asked, "What's wrong?" In tears, I told her about Clyde and our heated conversation. She started laughing. "Why don't you come out with me and the girls for awhile?" I was reluctant at first because I had abstained from alcohol for close to two years. Then I gave in. "Sure, why not?"

I drank enough to get tipsy and went directly home after closing time. For the first time in months, I had an enjoyable evening.

The next day, I felt rotten. I thought about the argument and knew it was wrong for of us to talk to each other that way. What hurt me the most was that Clyde had used our son to threaten me. About a week later, I got a letter from him. I never bothered to read it. I did the same with two letters that followed because I was fed up. I tore them up and watched the pieces float down the creek, wishing he would phone and talk to me properly. In the meantime, I continued with my counselling sessions. The counsellor noticed I was making progress and heading toward disclosure. He felt that, by the next visit, I might open up and discuss at least one experience.

Several weeks later, I got a registered letter. In bold print, it read, "legal separation." My knees buckled. I dropped to the floor and went into shock. I never thought Clyde would use such extreme measures to get to me. I tried to collect myself and walked over to the hospital to keep my counselling appointment. My counsellor noticed I was upset and asked, "Mary, what's wrong?" I broke down and handed him the document. "What are you going to do?" he asked.

"I don't know. There is Sean to consider."

He looked at me and asked, "Mary, why didn't you get help at the base?"

"Clyde would never have given me the support I needed. Like me, he has secrets he wants concealed." I took a deep breath and started crying again.

The counsellor said, "Mary, you know the saddest part of this whole ordeal? You love this man a lot!" I cried, knowing I did not have a chance of going home. This was the consequence of trying to escape my unresolved past.

The Family Breakdown

I told my parents Clyde had filed for a separation. They felt badly. My Dad got emotional and asked what I intended to do. Numbly, I responded, "I thought of going through with it. But it's not that easy. How did I allow things to get so bad?"

My Dad looked at me and said, "Hey! Don't blame yourself for everything. Do what you think is best."

"I know Clyde is serious. The only way I will cooperate is without formal legalities, even if it means I am to remain alone for the rest of my life." My parents were surprised with my decision and amazed I was trying to stay optimistic.

I cried that night and many nights after. I continued to go for counselling but this was a set back that forced the residential school issues aside. There was no sense disclosing them as I no longer had a military base to return to or a marriage to worry about. Even though Clyde intimidated me, I could not allow him to regain control of me. I went through the next few months in despair. Sometimes I drank to get drunk. I wanted to be sedated so I did not have to feel my heart ache. I wanted to be alone because I did not have any love to share. I wanted everyone who knew me to hate, curse, criticize, and beat me. I even wanted someone to kill me and put an end to my miserable existence.

The reality of being rejected and defeated by Clyde was not easy to accept. When Clyde got more heartless, I became harder. He noticed I would not give in so he decided withdraw his financial support for Sean. I decided to go back to school and support him myself, but in the meantime, resorted to drinking to dull the pain.

One evening, I met a couple—Ira and Danny—from Cold Lake, Alberta, who happened to know Clyde. I sat and drank with them. After a couple of hours of drinking, Ira turned on me. She said, "You're crazy to let a guy like Clyde get away. Actually," she continued, "you're stupid!"

I glared at her and answered, "This is none of your business!"

Ira ignored me. "Do you know what Clyde said about you?"

"I really don't care to know."

Danny noticed my irritation and said, "Mary's right. Leave her alone. There are two sides to every story."

Ira got angry. "She's got a nice husband."

I stood up, pushing my chair back roughly. "Lady," I said, "you don't even know me. If my husband is the saint you say he is, why the heck isn't he here?" I was still raw when it came to Clyde. I was so upset, I walked out and went to another bar. Later that evening, Ira and Danny found me. Ira seemed to gloat as she shared some interesting things about Clyde. Suddenly, I broke down as what she said pierced my heart. I knew then that my marriage was really over and had become polluted. Danny said, "Don't cry Mary! What goes around comes around." I had to get out. I wanted to be alone. I went to a motel room, crawled into bed, and cried until I passed out.

My drinking increased until my parents thought it was best I leave town. They took care of Sean and I went to stay with a relative in Thunder Bay. I was in poor health from all the stress. I had developed bad eating habits combined with the alcohol consumption and weighed only eighty pounds. After a few weeks, I was nursed back to health and began to show improvement. I went back to school to upgrade my education and sent money home for Sean.

About eighteen months into that time, separation documents were served to me. It was then I met Paul. We began dating and he moved in, but things did not work for us. Paul knew I was still very much in love with Clyde. He honestly said he could not compete and it put a tremendous strain on our relationship. "Mary, you're a classy lady," he said, "but all you can grant me is a dream. I know I can never keep you in my life unless you get over Clyde. Whenever you're ready, give me a call. I'll be there." I knew he was right. My feelings for Clyde were deep.

I went back home and returned to my old ways, shutting everyone out. In the process, my alcoholism became so bad, I could no longer care for my son. I turned on my parents who did nothing but support me in every possible way and put them through hell. I did not listen to the sound and wise advice they were giving. We got into a very bad argument and I was kicked out of the house and reported to the Children's Aid. Sean was taken away from me and placed under their guardianship. I got very angry. Vivian and I took off to Prince George, British Columbia. We got jobs as waitresses at Purden Lake Resort near Upper Fraser. After a few weeks, Vivian returned home. I stayed with my brother, George, who was going through a separation of his own. I helped with his children although alcoholism was still controlling me.

Then I got a letter from Children's Aid stating if I did not return for family court by a certain date, Sean was going to be placed for adoption. That snapped me back into reality and I realized I was abusing my son by failing to care for him and meet his needs. What I had said I would never do, I had done—become heartless and self-centered. I went back to Hearst to get my son and make amends with my parents. I learned to accept that my marriage was over. Although I had avoided the legal process, I had taken part in destroying and polluting the covenant I valued when I got involved with Paul. I regained custody of Sean and learned to appreciate the most precious and harmless human being in my life. I still drank but I knew I would have to let go of it sooner or later.

One evening, after drinking in the bars, I came to an alleyway and sat down on a step. I felt so lonely, I started crying. I did not want to be alone and longed for someone to share my life with, someone who would accept my son, someone who would love me unconditionally. In desperation, I prayed, "God, you've heard from me before. Perhaps I do not deserve to ask anything of you. But I want someone special in my life to care for Sean and me because I can't do it alone." I wiped my tears and walked away.

I came to a restaurant. My brothers, Peter and Fred, were sitting with a friend. They invited me to join them and introduced me to Terry. Normally, I would have sat and talked for awhile and left. But Terry spoke up and said, "Do you want to party with me?" I looked at him and debated the idea. "I won't do anything to you. I just want someone to hang around with," he added.

I replied, "Oh, okay," figuring he was all right or my brothers would have warned me.

We really enjoyed one another's company from the day we met. Terry and I became good friends and started seeing each other frequently. We both agreed not to get emotionally involved and accepted each other as good friends. True to our word, we parted as friends.

Terry contacted me whenever he came to town. I gradually became interested in him because he was different. He was easygoing and did not expect anything of me. He was considerate and sensitive to my feelings. He was attentive and cautious in how he handled my emotions. He did not force me to make any decisions but allowed me to move at my pace. He was a gentleman, not a chauvinist. I was uncertain at first, simply because the qualities he possessed were rare.

I met other guys, but no one could hold my attention and impress me like Terry. Prior to him, I never thought such qualities existed outside fairytales. I was not really an affectionate type, but I noticed Terry appreciated a hug. He really captivated me. We worked on our relationship and soon became a twosome. I noticed I was no longer interested in finding someone to share my life.

Terry filled that void completely. However, I still had a habit of sheltering my feelings and protecting myself by keeping my distance.

One evening, while Terry and I were out, a young lady expressed interest in him. I told her he was a bachelor and available. Terry did not respond to the flirting at first, but eventually started paying attention to Sheila. That evening, I experienced a new feeling—jealousy. I thought there was something wrong with me and suddenly wanted to get out of this relationship that I had begun to treasure. I wanted to run.

Instead, I followed Sheila into the bathroom and waited for her to sit down. When she least expected it, I kicked in the stall door and pulled her out by the hair. I banged her head back and forth between the cubical walls, got her to her knees, and bent her over the toilet. She was stunned. "Don't ever flirt with my boyfriend again!" I shouted.

"Okay, Mary, I won't. Just let go of me!" I left her in the bathroom. She came back out to sit with us but was soaking wet and did not even look at Terry.

That same evening, I knew Clyde was going to come after me with a final blow. I felt staring eyes and there were Ira and Danny. I knew they were going to report back to Clyde that I finally did have someone in my life. This time it was different; I was prepared and expected to hear from him. My intuition was accurate. I had managed to avoid the legalities for two years, but now Clyde got his lawyer to serve me with divorce papers through a deputy sheriff. He was terminating our marriage permanently. The sheriff said, "Mary, I have been searching for you. Do you have all the legal documents that have been sent to you?"

"Yes. I did not want to go through the legal system," I replied.

"That's understandable, but he has changed his grounds to irreconcilable differences instead of all that nonsense he was accusing you of. Take them to a lawyer and protect yourself. Give the sucker his divorce." I started laughing. He handed me the petition for a divorce decree and instructed me where to sign. Once again, I felt powerless and helpless. After the deputy left, I went for a walk to the bridge. For the first time, I allowed myself to grieve for my marriage and family breakdown. Clyde must have thought he had won, but no one wins under such circumstances. I concluded that we were very immature adults and irresponsible parents who victimized our son through our actions.

Poisonous Mary

I became more relaxed once I accepted where I stood with Clyde. I went to a lawyer and gave him all the legal documents I'd collected for two years. As he read them, he was surprised by the unreasonable requests and charges Clyde had file against me. "Why didn't you fight back?" he asked.

"It wasn't worth it. I have a son and that's all I wanted."

"Your former husband is getting off easy. You have the right to go after him for half of his assets."

"I know," I replied. "I just don't want to stoop to his level."

"Are you sure you don't want to pursue it?" he asked.

"No. He has made me feel like a fugitive for the past two years. I'm tired."

"Mary, at least go for child support. How does $125 a month until Sean turns eighteen sound?"

"Why not? That's not like asking for an arm and a

leg, is it? I would like to see him raise our son with that amount."

"Mary," said Mr. Burns compassionately, "I wish I had more cases like yours. It's nice to see you trying to be civil. But it's sad to see him take advantage of you." Once he completed sorting though the documents, the majority were discarded. "Most important is his request for a divorce," he told me. I signed. As I got up to leave, Mr. Burns followed me to the door. "It's okay to hurt, you know."

I nodded my head. "Yeah, I know. Thank you for everything!"

I left that office feeling like Clyde had buried me alive. I was emotionally numb and mentally drained. For the next few weeks, I felt terrible. Terry came around more frequently and I wondered how it was possible he wanted to associate with me. Did he know I was going through a divorce? Terry knew I was feeling down and was worried about me. He made it perfectly clear he was accepting me unconditionally. "Hon, I know this is premature," he said, "but why don't you and Sean come and spend a few days at my place? I'll take care of both of you, no strings attached!"

"I don't know what to think or how I should feel."

"That must be a normal phase. You are leaving a relationship permanently. Maybe a change of scenery will do you good." I was amazed by his attitude. Moreover, Sean seemed to approve of Terry, and I was pleased they liked each other. I agreed. After several days of limbo, I snapped out of it. Terry was right. It did me good to get away.

One night, however, I woke up screaming and crying. Terry held me and said, "It's okay, hon. No one can hurt you anymore. You are having one of your bad nightmares." He talked to me gently until I became calm. For many nights afterwards, I thought my heart was going to stop. I had been so preoccupied with Clyde, I'd managed to keep my residential school experiences under control. It dawned on me that night that it felt good to be cared for and treated like a human being. I had developed a habit of ignoring my fears and neglecting myself. I vowed no one was going to beat me again, drunk or sober.

Several months after the divorce became final, Terry and I decided to live together. He had nominated himself to take me on with all my flaws and faults. I felt secure with him and knew Sean and I were in good hands. We lived in Oba until Sean started going to school in Hearst.

Terry was patient with me. The nightmares came and went. Sometimes, my memories were overwhelming and I would break down and cry uncontrollably. Other times, I would go out and get drunk. Even though it was an unhealthy way to deal with my pain, it was temporary relief from the pressures. Terry always suspected my negative behaviour stemmed from traumatic experiences. He found two ways to help me. He always embraced me when I cried. Even when I struggled to push him away, he would cling to me until I surrendered and allowed myself to be held. And he never forced me to talk about what was bothering me. He would just let me cry and would say, "It's okay. It will come out sooner or later. Take your time. I'm here for you."

My drinking had increased excessively prior to the divorce. When Terry became involved, it decreased. I had some normalcy in my life but was still on shaky ground. When Terry and I drank, we always made sure Sean was well taken care of. We got into a few scuffles. I walked out on him and stuck to my vow that no one was going to violate me again.

Four years into our relationship, I had marked my boundary lines without being completely rigid. I learned to compromise constructively. I was beginning to identify my problem and find solutions. Terry and I got along exceptionally well without alcohol. When we did drink together, we promised not to fight. I made breakthroughs when I stopped stuffing things within and started feeling and dealing with the pain. I started to look at my negative and inappropriate behaviours and identified the areas that needed improvement.

Unfortunately, because of my excessive drinking, I hurt my siblings many times. This often happened when I was intoxicated but that was no excuse. I had no right to hurt anyone. One day, one of my brothers came to me and said I had been labelled "Poisonous Mary" by another family member. I was flattered at first because it described me. I wanted everyone to know I was tough and unfeeling. Over time, however, the name made me look at myself and I didn't like what I saw. But no one knew of the recipe I had written several years after residential school, called the "Poisonous Mary" It went something like this:

8 cups of denial   *7 days of secrecy*
5 cups of shame/guilt   *7 cups of hate*
6 cups of no trust   *2 buckets of tears*
3 blocks of crushed ice   *4 cups of anger*
5 teaspoons of bittersweet lemon
1 Tablet of tranquilizer (for sleep or for nerves)

Blend crushed ice, bittersweet lemon; add denial, shame/guilt, anger and hate. Divide into two portions; place half in a corner of the brain. Take the remainder and pat around the heart until it hardens and forms a a crust. Apply with secrecy and no trust. Glaze with two buckets of tears. Should secrets begin to seep through the heart and mind, garnish with sleeping or nerve tranquilizer. Should symptoms persist, go on a three-day binge and overdose on alcohol.

It was the only way I knew how to cope with the painful memories. The problem was, alcohol was destroying me. I would black out and not remember a thing. By this time, Terry had quit drinking. He wanted our relationship to work. I want both—the relationship and the alcohol. I continued to drink but was running out of excuses. In the end, all I said was, "I'm following my ancestors!"

One day, Terry said, "That's it! I've had it! It's either me or the booze!" I got insulted and thought, "How dare he give me an ultimatum?" I picked up my jacket and walked out the door.

"When you get back, I won't be here!" he yelled after me. I ignored him and kept walking. But something odd happened in that dispute. I began to show signs of a conscience. "Mary, do you realize what you just did back there?" I asked myself. "You just chose booze over someone that cares about you a lot. Terry has been faithfully supporting you. What is the matter with you, girl?" Apologies were not in my vocabulary... yet. But then I got emotional and asked myself, "Aren't you tired of running around the same circle?" I acknowledged my fondness for

Terry and knew alcohol was putting a strain on our relationship. I considered religion, too. Why was it not as important to me as it used to be? Questions kept haunting me. Was there was a Jesus? Did he really come for people like me? I was determined to get some answers.

I stopped at the Roman Catholic Church in town where I had decided to speak with a priest. He looked as if he was in a hurry. "Can you explain whether or not Jesus existed?" I asked.

"What church do you go to?" he returned.

"I'm Roman Catholic but, since the divorce...."

The priest looked at me and said, "You know you've lost all your rights according to our church laws?" I looked at him and wondered what my question had to do with my personal life. "In other words, you're excommunicated from the Roman Catholic Church." Which also meant he did not even have to talk with me.

I was stunned that he was so blunt about it. I looked at him and said, "I just wanted to know about...."

"I'm busy. I have to go."

I was dissatisfied that my question was left unanswered. I started walking down the street and came to the Pentecostal Church. Daniel, one of the people that attended the church, was sitting on the bench. "Hi Daniel," I said. "Is there a head person I could speak to?"

"Mary, you're a drunk! Your involvement with this church would give us a bad reputation." I was at a loss for words.

I continued walking down the street and stopped at an Anglican Church. The door was locked. I sat on the step and said, "I guess there's no Jesus. I may as well go where I belong," and headed to the bar.

My friend Derek was there. "You know, Mary," he said, "you don't belong here. Why don't you get out while you can. You're a decent woman. If you continue with this scene, you're going to end up like them." I looked over and saw how fast the girls I usually drank with were deteriorating. "Do you want to end up with that type of a reputation?" he asked.

"No. I just don't know how to get out of it."

"Sure you do. Terry loves you a lot."

"I think he left me."

"Terry? Nah! He'll come for you."

"I don't know. I made a really stupid decision back there."

"Hang around. Terry will show up; I know him. He won't let you go that easy!"

On my second day of drinking, I sat staring at the floor. Suddenly, I noticed a familiar pair of runners. I looked up slowly and said, "Terry! I thought you left."

"No hon," he said. "Are you coming home?"

"No! This is where I belong." Terry looked at me. He picked me up and carried me right out of the bar. I kept saying, "Terry, you have to go on without me. You need to go on with your life. Please Terry, let me go!"

"No hon. I love you," he answered.

"Terry, I'm no good for you."

"Hon, I love you."

"Terry, I don't think I could ever love anyone again!"

"It's okay, hon. I'll wait for you."

I began crying and sobbing, "I can't go on like this!"

"Hon, I'll give you something to eat. Then you're going to get some sleep. And we're going to have our bar-becue with Sean as planned." I remember looking at him, thinking, "Is this guy for real? He hasn't heard a word I've said and he's talking about a barbecue!"

We got to the house and I sat at the table, numb. I remember looking at a knife. I grabbed it and said, "I would be better off dead! I can't go on!" Terry came towards me. For a split second, Sister Deanna appeared with her grin. I wanted to get away. It was too real. Terry and I fell to the floor as we struggled. He kept saying, "Hon, give me the knife! You're going to hurt yourself! Hon! I love you. I love you. Give me the knife." Then he yelled it—"Hon, I love you!"

I started to weep. "Terry! I'm an alcoholic! I'm an alcoholic!" He embraced me with both arms and started rocking me. The emotion he expressed that day penetrated the circle I had built around my heart. "It's okay, hon," he said. "I'm going to help you. We're going to get through this together. I love you. I'm not going to leave you!" For the first time in years, I allowed myself to feel the love of another person. I wept in desperation from my heart. Even though I stunk of booze, Terry still took me in his arms and held me until I passed out.

Regaining Control

When I awoke late that afternoon, I was depressed and had a very bad hangover. I sat on my bed and wept. "God are you really there?" I sobbed. "Please help me! I cannot go on this way." I wiped my tears and went into the kitchen to get some juice.

Terry was happy to see me. "Hi babe!" he said. I gave him an unenthusiastic "Hi." After drinking my juice, I walked out the door and down the road. Terry came running after me. "Hon, where are you going?"

"Back to town."

He looked at me and said, "No, hon, you're not."

"Terry, I have to go."

He approached me and took me in his arms. "Come on. Let's go home." I began crying and I could not understand why he cared for me so much or why I was responding to him. The fear of taking another chance at another serious relationship was overwhelming. That day, I knew my past had completely caught up with me.

I felt in such despair and beyond repair. Everything seemed to come to a standstill. I knew there was no more sense in running. Everything my physical eyes looked at seemed gray and bleak. Terry knew there was something different about me, and broke the silence by saying, "Hon, we will get through this together."

I nervously replied, "I hope so." I wanted to say more but Terry interrupted me.

"Hon, why don't you cut the vegetables for our salad?"

"Huh? Salad?" I recall thinking, "Does this guy see the seriousness of my state?" But I went ahead and cut the vegetables. There was a knock at the door. "Come in," I said, but there was no response. I continued cutting. I heard a second knock which was a little harder and again, said, "Come in!" Still no response. "Probably the kids fooling around," I thought. Then came a third still-louder knock. "Come in!!" I yelled. I dropped my knife and held my hands to my head. I had such a bad hangover that when I raised my voice, I thought my head was going to split open. The door opened and there stood a tall man. He said, "Hi! My name is Brother Wally. I'm an evangelist from BC."

"What's an evangelist?" I asked.

"A preacher. Does anyone here need help?"

"With what?" I asked.

"Better still, has anyone here asked God for help?" My mouth fell open. I did not know what to think. Then I became angry, and said, "I don't want to talk about God. Do you realize I was turned away from two churches and locked out of another?"

He looked concerned. "What's your name?"

"Mary."

He sat down on a chair and said, "Can I sit and talk with you?"

"Yeah, I guess so." I was thinking, *"Man! This man has guts!"*

"You know, Mary," he continued, "denomination and spirituality are two different topics."

"What do you mean?"

"A denomination is the type of church a person belongs to and attends regularly. Spirituality is accepting Jesus into your heart and having a personal relationship with him."

"How could Jesus want me when I'm the biggest scum to walk the earth?" I countered angrily. Within a few seconds, I began weeping, and said, "There is no Jesus. I went to look for him and I could not find him."

"Mary, you're spiritually bankrupt."

I felt insulted. "What are you talking about?"

"Jesus wants you to accept him as your savior."

"How do you know that?"

"You have to accept him by faith."

"What's that?"

"Believing with all your heart that he is the Son of God who died for your sins and rose from the dead."

By this time, I was upset. I wanted to throw him out. Sobbing, I said, "I don't want to listen to this. I hate myself. I feel so very, very ugly. I don't want this. I'm nothing but an alcoholic."

"You know, Mary," he said empathetically, "I was an alcoholic. Jesus helped me and took it away."

I looked at him in disbelief. "Yeah, right!" I wanted him to leave because the conversation was getting too much for me. What amazed me, was that, during our short encounter, he got me to express myself.

Suddenly, he asked, "Mary, may I pray for you?"

"Yes," I replied, but only because I wanted to get rid of him. I thought it was better than throwing him out. As he got up, I said, "Thank...," but before I finished what I wanted to say, he laid his hands on my head and said, "Mary, repeat after me. Father, I come to you in the name of Jesus. I ask you to forgive me for all my sins. Cleanse me with the blood of Jesus that flowed freely for me. Come into my heart as my Lord and Savior. Amen."

Then he continued the prayer on his own. "Father, I come to you in the name of Jesus, asking you to set Mary free from any suicidal thoughts. Restore and renew life in her. Heal Mary from all the abuses she has experienced in her life. I ask that you set her free from alcoholism from this day forward in Jesus' name. Amen." I cried through the entire prayer. A sensation of peace and tranquility took root in my spirit. I felt clean and a freedom bubbled within. Before Brother Wally left, he said, "Mary, you will run into problems but you will be able to handle them better."

From that day forward, I never had the desire to drink alcohol again. At first, I became super religious, but in the end, learned to respect different ways of praying. I learned to live by applying the spiritual beliefs found in my Bible. Terry and I gave our lives to God. It was the beginning of a new inspirational life under God's loving grace. In the process, God helped me gain control of my life.

Shortly after accepting and understanding spirituality, I came to terms with my residential school experiences. I continued to work at it and got rid of the bitterness in my spirit. I longed for peace in my heart and soul. For years, I had kept myself unhealthy by concealing secrets. But no matter where I ran, I always came to a dead end. The violations of my victimization were always there to greet me. I was motivated to take a deeper look at myself because I couldn't stand being called Poisonous Mary.

My son showed me there was no shame in having feelings and expressing them. I remember looking at him and admiring the tears that rolled down his chubby cheeks. He explained how he felt when he fell off his bike and skinned his knee. To him, it was important to express his hurt because he knew his pain was genuine. As he cried and talked, I took him in my arms and embraced him. The instant I consoled him, the memory of a beaten girl that I had placed inside a rose years before, budded open. That little girl was me! I became emotional and teary-eyed. Suddenly, Sean looked at me and said, "Don't cry, Mommy, you big baby!" I started laughing as I gave him a hug. Sean was not aware that his tears watered the roots of my healing.

Terry bravely challenged me through many battles, and won. He saw in me a person worth fighting for and nurtured her with unconditional love and acceptance, understanding, listening, comforting, and encouraging constantly.

In the end, it was really me that needed to do the work within myself. I took the risk of unlocking the secret abuses I had experienced at the residential school. I let all the memories out: the two Native nuns, my supervisors, who used excessive strength to beat me; the harsh and inhumane tactics used to mold me; the degradation of having my hair cut publicly; watching other girls beaten senseless; nuns who enforced the suppression of my emotions; the decimation of my individuality; the white nun, my teacher, who showed me it was okay to lie, cheat, and steal, to verbally abuse people, to make others feel useless and worthless; the priest who belittled my ancestry with stories of Bambo, causing me to believe I could go to hell because I was Native, and who violated me and blamed me for "tempting" him; adult "role models" who wore habits and robes and reflected negative and inappropriate behaviour, abusing their positions and authority.

The pictures flashed across my mind's eye. My delicate, youthful mind had been damaged, my body scarred with bruises, my spirit wounded. And it all started when I was only nine years old.

Taking the Girl Out of the Rose

I took little Mary out of the rose because I soon came to realize that, although roses smell beautiful and are pretty to look at, they have thorns. I never realized I had used a survival technique for my own protection, to maintain my sanity, to escape the reality of my pain, and to conceal the abuses I was subjected to. My cognitive capacity was not allowed to expand because my caregivers used it to condition me with fear. Even though I struggled with personal growth, I gradually dealt with each abuse as it arose and began to heal.

I learned it was normal to have feelings. I grieved the loss of my childhood, the shattered bond with my parents and siblings, and the personal losses of my youth and adulthood. Recovery increased when I took responsibility for my own inappropriate behaviour and unwise decisions and stopped blaming my failures on my abusers. I became wiser. When I evaluated the hate I felt for my abusers, I was able to admit it did not apply to all nuns and priests. In fact, it did not even apply to the ones who afflicted so much pain and grief on my life. What I hated were the abuses and violations themselves. I could forgive my abusers.

I also had to realize I was not Super Mary. God granted me humility. When I stopped running, he granted me awareness and courage. When I stopped concealing my painful secrets, I learned to feel. My tunnel vision broadened.

As I traveled through my healing journey, I came to a fork in the road; one path was constructive, the other destructive, and the choice was entirely up to me. I was able to chose the right way because when I learned to communicate, I learned to disclose. When I disclosed, I finally found closure and began to live and looked forward to a brighter future.

When I evaluated my relationship with my son, I had to admit I was not a perfect parent. Many times I wished he had been born with a manual. I learned to give him what I had lacked as a child. Then I poured on love and care, and sought to meet all his personal needs. I was honest with Sean about his biological father when the day I had most been dreading arrived, and Sean asked, "Mommy, why did my father divorce you?"

Very carefully, I replied, "Sean, we were young, naive and very unhappy. We both thought it was the best thing to do. I'm sorry it ended up this way because we made a decision in which you were trapped. You were not to blame. You're my pride and joy and the best thing I have to show for my life." I had promised myself I would not create a negative image of his biological parent. Sean had the right to find out for himself.

As he was growing, there were two things I needed to give him. The first was a strong foundation of morals and values. The second was independence. I learned to respect who him and teach him to build strong boundaries. Open communication was the key to strengthening our relationship and directing him on the path to a meaningful life.

Shortly after the healing began, Terry and I got married. Then we encountered a serious problem. The polymiocitis I was diagnosed with in 1975 returned with a vengeance. It affected the main muscles on my shoulders and hips, taking my mobility in the process. I was completely out of commission. A disabled person's life is not as easy as it's portrayed on television. I went from a vibrant and active person to a complete invalid. All I was able to do at the time was move my head, shift my eyeballs, and exercise my lungs by crying and screaming. I gave Terry the option of leaving because I felt it was unfair to expect him to live with me in my condition. Terry flatly refused and chose not to give up on me.

So many times, I got frustrated because I could not do the normal things I used to. Feeding myself, brushing my teeth, combing my hair—they all exhausted me. I lost my privacy in the inability to go to the bathroom or have a bath by myself. I had to wait for Terry to assist me. A few times, I had accidents in my bed. I thought I would have a mental breakdown when it happened. I would be so upset and cry. Terry, in his loving way, would say, "It's okay, hon. I'll help you. All you need is a bath and a change of linen. While he was cleaning me, he would say, "It's okay, hon! You can't help it. I love you, hon. I love you."

One day, I told Terry to go back to work. I insisted I was strong enough to stay home alone. Shortly after he left, I got cramps. I thought I would get up and try to walk. I took a step forward and went crashing to the floor. I could not get up. I ended up messing my pants and stayed in that state all day until Terry got home. We were both so upset, we cried together. He said, "It's okay, hon. I'll help you. All you need is a bath and a change of clothes."

Terry totally amazed me by adapting to my changed lifestyle. Sometimes, the grieving was severe. On a very hard day, I found strength to push my plate of food to the floor. I acted like a spoiled brat. Terry would clean it up. Then I would feel guilty because he took it so well. One day, Terry said he had had enough, and I thought he was leaving. Instead, he got me dressed while I struggled and gave him a hard time. After several months of being in the house, he was taking me out. Once he got my coat on, he literally carried me out the door. No matter how much I protested and cried, he would not take me back. It hurt him to ignore me and he showed he was listening by kissing my forehead. This became a routine until I got used to it. Terry would not give up on me.

Eventually, I had to accept my limitations and restrictions. I picked up some crafts. Terry and I got involved in volunteer work and politics in the community of Hearst. I became president of the local Ontario Metis and Non-Status Association, and Terry became the treasurer. We worked as a team and became outspoken advocates on Native issues. Together, we got the geared-to-income housing for Natives in Hearst.

I even adapted to my wheelchair. I learned to be grateful that I had more than other people with disabilities. When I felt angry or full of self pity, I always met someone with a more severe condition. At least I was able to see and hear and had all my limbs.

Later, Terry and I dropped politics and enrolled as mature students at Northern College in the Native Drug and Alcohol Program. When we started, there were eleven students. Throughout the year, some dropped out while others extended their terms. Terry and I worked away, enduring all the hardships that came with it. In 1989, we were the only two graduates from our class. There were times I wanted to quit. The workload was tremendous. But my husband and I knew we could make it together. I was so thankful to have Rachelle Piche as my instructor. She saw my potential, overlooked my disability, and encouraged me in my abilities.

Although I never did get a job, it was worth my time and effort to fulfill the dream of becoming a counsellor. I became very assertive and learned to speak against discrimination. I accepted two appointments from the NDP government: the Ontario Advisory Council for People with Disabilities and the Ontario Human Rights Task Force. Terry got employment at the Jubilee Treatment Center. He worked hard as attendant, counsellor, and unit supervisor, and today has become Director of Counselling.

My sister, Vivian, graduated as a Health Development Worker. Peter graduated as a Drug and Alcohol Counsellor. Edmond and Johnny graduated as Microcomputer Business Administrators. Fred became a foreman for Fontaine in Calstock and is presently a Council member for Constance Lake Reservation. George is a labourer for a sawmill in Upper Fraser and resides in Prince George, BC. Teresa resides in Thunder Bay. Michael is continuing to work on himself and resides in Toronto. Mother now has eleven children, twenty-three grandchildren, and fifteen great-grand children. Sadly, in the past few years, Margaret, James, and Dad all passed away.

Through all my experiences, I became a stronger person with an improved attitude. I put my past to rest and chose to heal. I had entered the residential school system as a little girl already showing symptoms of generational problems. I enrolled to be cared for and was betrayed in every possible way. As I got older, my growth was stunted by the unresolved abuses that followed me into adulthood. But my healing journey taught me about the negative impact of the residential school system and I gained an understanding of how things came to be. I learned to say, without any shame, "I was a victim." Before long, I was able to say, "I'm a survivor." Now, I'm proud to say, "I'm a conqueror!"

Appendix A

Operations at St. Ann's

There was no orientation or written schedule distributed upon admission to St. Ann's, but I managed to adapt by imitating others in the following practices and guidelines:

1. Students were separated into four groups upon admission according to gender and age.

2. Students were assigned a supervisor according to gender, then given:
   - a number
   - a shower and hair treatment for lice
   - a Robin-Hood style haircut
   - a uniform (jumper, blouse, sweater, slip, undershirt, bloomers and stockings with marked identification numbers inside each article).

3. Designated student areas:
   - recreation room
   - dormitory
   - cafeteria
   - chapel
   - outside: invisible boundaries for younger girls, chain-link fenced area for older boys and older girls.

4. Students were given supervised weekly showers at which:
   - full-sized apron garment was worn
   - uniforms and undergarments were changed.

5. Regulated rules:
   - Students were to remain with supervisor and group at all times.
   - Students were not permitted to talk in halls, cafeteria, or dormitory.
   - Students were not to acknowledge or speak to siblings from other groups.
   - In-coming letters were censored prior to distribution; out-going letters were censored prior to being sealed.
   - Parcels were opened and inspected when received and kept in the office.

6. Non-verbal cues:
   - The wake-up call was the sound of a manual school bell used by the supervisor.
   - Two claps indicated students were to form a line and follow the supervisor in silence.
   - A wooden clapper used by Sister Superior had various meanings: one click meant stand or sit; two

clicks meant kneel and two more clicks meant stand.

- At the completion of Mass, we were trained to stand and wait for the supervisor and then follow her in silence.

7. Daily operations:
   - Wake up call, get on knees and pray
   - Wash up, get dressed, make up bed in silence
   - Pray, breakfast in cafeteria, pray
   - Return to recreation room, wait for class or do assigned chores prior to going to class
   - During class: pray, religion, arithmetic, writing, reading, a little history, geography, and silence
   - Recess: repeated loop of walking out one classroom door and entering the other
   - Lunch: pray, eat, pray, and return to cafeteria until class time
   - Mid-afternoon recess: repeat morning recess
   - Return to recreation room, play, talk
   - Dinner: pray, eat, pray, return to recreation room, play, talk, occasional play time outside in designated areas
   - Bedtime: pray, undress in silence, go to washroom, go to bed.

8. Weekend schedule:

Students from the village went home except at spring break-up; the reminder stayed at the school, usually on the premises. The girls were allowed to play with toys that were normally locked away or taught to darn and mend socks.

9. Social activities over the course of two years:
  - five movies
  - one visit with siblings
  - one Winter Carnival
  - three weekends at a girl's camp
  - one staff-supervised co-ed dance
  - one floor hockey competition.

10. Annual official visits:

I was present for two annual visits from government officials, and many amendments were made to normal school routine.

  - Formal uniforms were distributed: burgundy jumpers and white blouses for girls, navy blazers, light blue shirt, and gray trousers for boys.
  - Students stood outside and greeted the guests by singing the St. Anne's theme as they walked up a red carpet.
  - Menus were changed; turkey, mashed potatoes, gravy, vegetables, and ice cream were served.
  - Students were permitted to speak during dinner and dine with all groups as well as staff.
  - Social activities were organized by students: younger boys and girls sang; older boys and girls demonstrated Boy Scout and Girl Guides skills; the winner from each group presented speaking contest speech; boys and girls played band instruments and were bribed with money to pay attention—I know because I made fifteen cents!

Once the guests were gone, we returned to normal uniforms, a basic menu, silence rules, and our rigid schedule.

Appendix B

Child Hidden in a Rose

I exist in a cold brick building,
Far from home and family.
I dwell with girls that are a part of my being;
I function like a puppet on a string.

I am a child living in a military setting,
Detained and groomed into a rigid routine.
An open target I've become
To teachers with a mission and a scheme.

My mind is blended with guilt and shame
That no child should ever know.
My heart is covered with sores and a stench
That only I can smell.

My body is bruised and battered.
Once free to let my tears and fears flow,

I'm now locked inside myself,
Forbidden to let my heart show.

The only way I can be seen
Is with my mask and plastic smile.
No one knows it is me
Under this one-sized costume, worn by all.

Punishment is the daily norm,
So I've hidden in a rose to escape the scorn.
It's been a haven, a place of fantasy,
An escape from life to maintain my sanity.

But when the rose begins to bloom,
The child snuggled in that flowery room
Is afraid to come out but yearns to heal
From the painful secrets she has learned to conceal.

Day by day, her strength she gains,
And 'though the rose is scented and safe,
She sees its thorns and frees herself from the rose
That helped her survive so many years ago.